stopwatch

Student's Book
& Workbook

3

Alastair Lane

Richmond

58 St Aldates
Oxford
OX1 1ST
United Kingdom

Stopwatch Student's Book Level 3

First Edition: January 2016
ISBN: 978-607-06-1241-1

© Text: Alastair Lane
© Richmond Publishing, S.A. de C.V. 2016
Av. Río Mixcoac No. 274, Col. Acacias,
Del. Benito Juárez, C.P. 03240, México, D.F.

Publisher: Justine Piekarowicz
Editorial Team: Daniel Altamirano, Suzanne Guerrero, Kimberly MacCurdy, Joep van der Werff
Art and Design Coordinators: Jaime Angeles, Karla Avila
Design: Jaime Angeles
Layout: Jaime Angeles, Daniel Mejĺa
Pre-Press Coordinator: Daniel Santillán
Pre-Press Team: Susana Alcántara, Virginia Arroyo
Cover Design: Karla Avila
Cover Photograph: © **Thinkstock:** saintho (Group yacht at regatta)

Illustrations: Fabián de Jesús Ramírez pp.: 58, 62, 63; Ismael Vázquez pp.: 15, 25, 30, 31, 38, 44, 45, 57, 73, 75, 86, 87, 98, 99, 100, 101, 108, 112, 113, 115, 122, 126, 130, 142, 143, 144.

Photographs: © **AFP:** CDSB / IMAGINECHINA p. 53 (center), MARTIN BERNETTI / AFP p. 90 (bottom), PETER STEFFEN / DPA / DPA PICTURE-ALLIANCE/AFP p. 148 (center right), GARRICK CLUB / THE ART ARCHIVE / THE PICTURE DESK p. 149 (right), AMBLIN ENTERTAINMENT / CHINA FIL / COLLECTION CHRISTOPHEL p. 116 (ex. 1, left and right); © **AAPIMAGE:** AAP Image/Lukas Coch pp. (all): 102. © **Christoph_Otto** pp. 18-19. © **Shutterstock.com** jack_photo p. 13 (three symbols on a fence), Michel Stevelmans p. 31 (traffic jam), pio3 p. 38 (Times Square), Albert Pego p. 39 (Canon City), ChameleonsEye p. 39 (taxi cab), CaseyMartin p. 40 (airport), serato p. 40 (cockpit), Barone Firenze p. 41 (Xbox 360 and Kinect), Hadrian p. 41 (smartwatch), Chris Harvey p. 45 (cosplayers), Rob Wilson p. 62 (white Garbage Truck), Elzbieta Sekowska p. 72 (classmates, family party), KUCO p. 72 (man), Iakov Filimonov p. 75 (bottom right), Kamira p. 75 (bottom center), Crystal Home p. 75 (bottom left), Nacho Such p. 77 (bedouin family), haziafolio p. 80 (board game), Rob Hainer p. 82 (board game pieces), manaemedia p. 88 (tablet and cell phone), Panutphong p. 88 (ipod classic), Rose Carson p. 88 (Apple logo), SGM p. 88 (Apple iMac), Jaguar PS p. 88 (*Toy Story* stars), Jaguar PS p. 89 (Steve Jobs), eskay p. 93 (soda cans), Richard Thornton p. 112 (high school), Elena Dijour p. 112 (vendor), Joseph Sohmp 113 (Little League Field), Mikadun p. 119 (Holi festival, center and bottom), chrisdorney p. 119 (TripAdvisor website), domhnall dods pp. 120, 121 (military tattoo), Neftali p. 121 (stamp), Cornfield p. 121 (sign), Joseph Sohm p. 129 (school children), Taina Sohlman p. 130 (fire engine), Matt Gibson p. 130 (airshow), Ju1978 p. 130 (car factory), Alexey Boldin p. 142 (Facebook timeline), Saman527 p. 144 (interior, top), Eddy Galeotti p. 145 (Campeche, Mexico), Twocoms p. 155 (promoting Dr. Who), tanuha2001 p. 156 (Twitter logotype), catwalker p. 157 (stamp).

© **Wikipedia** (Robert Louis Stevenson, public domain) p. 149

Images used under license from © **Shutterstock.com** and © **Thinkstock.com**.

All rights reserved. No part of this work may be reproduced, stored in a retrieval system or transmitted in any form or by any means without prior written permission from the Publisher.

Richmond publications may contain links to third party websites or apps. We have no control over the content of these websites or apps, which may change frequently, and we are not responsible for the content or the way it may be used with our materials. Teachers and students are advised to exercise discretion when accessing the links.

The Publisher has made every effort to trace the owner of copyright material; however, the Publisher will correct any involuntary omission at the earliest opportunity.

Printed in Brazil by Forma Certa
Lote: 769726
Cod.: 292712411
2022

Contents

Student's Book

- 4 — Scope and Sequence
- 7 — Unit 0 — Can learning be fun?
- 13 — Unit 1 — Why do we need rules?
- 27 — Unit 2 — What's the best job?
- 41 — Unit 3 — Do we really need all this stuff?
- 55 — Unit 4 — How do you protect the planet?
- 69 — Unit 5 — What does it mean to be happy?
- 83 — Unit 6 — Where do bright ideas come from?
- 97 — Unit 7 — When is the right time?
- 111 — Unit 8 — How do you feel?

Workbook

- 126 — Unit 1
- 130 — Unit 2
- 134 — Unit 3
- 138 — Unit 4
- 142 — Unit 5
- 146 — Unit 6
- 150 — Unit 7
- 154 — Unit 8

- 158 — Just for Fun Answer Key
- 159 — Grammar Reference
- 168 — Verb List

Scope and Sequence

Unit	Vocabulary	Grammar	Skills
0 Can learning be fun?	**Review:** rooms in a house, furniture, classroom objects, food, clothes, free-time activities	Verb *be*; *There is / are*; *Can*; Imperatives	**Reading:** Identifying the main idea
1 Why do we need rules?	**School Supplies:** calculator, dictionary, gym uniform, recorder, ruler, sneakers **School Subjects:** art, chemistry, English, geography, history, literature, math, music, physical education, Spanish, technology	Present simple; Adverbs of frequency: *always, never, often, sometimes, usually*; Prepositions of time: *in, on, at*	**Listening:** Identifying key words **Writing:** Describing one's morning routine **Project:** Creating an infographic
2 What's the best job?	**Jobs:** engineer, firefighter, hairstylist, pilot, receptionist, transit operator **Workplaces:** airport, factory, fire station, hotel, salon, train station	Present continuous; Prepositions of place: *on, at, in*	**Reading:** Identifying and distinguishing facts from opinions **Writing:** Describing an imaginary job **Project:** Researching and writing about a dream job
3 Do we really need all this stuff?	**Clothes:** belt, blouse, coat, dress, hat, jeans, jewelry, pants, scarf, shorts, skirt, sneakers, socks, sweater, T-shirt	Comparative and superlative adjectives	**Reading:** Skimming and scanning **Listening:** Identifying specific information **Project:** Designing a bulletin board
4 How do you protect the planet?	**Food:** apple, bread, carrot, flour, lettuce, lime, milk, onion, orange, salami, strawberry, sugar, potato, tomato	Countable and uncountable nouns; Quantifiers: *a lot of, some, a little, a few, any*; *How much, How many*	**Writing:** Organizing ideas in paragraphs **Speaking:** Interviewing a classmate **Project:** Creating a short video to promote a green attitude

Unit	Vocabulary	Grammar	Skills
5 **What does it mean to be happy?**	**Pastimes:** camping, dancing, doing cannonballs, drawing, hanging out with friends, making models, playing board games, popping a wheelie, rollerblading	Verb *be: was, were*; *There was / were* Short answers	**Reading:** Describing a photo **Speaking:** Describing a photo **Project:** Designing and conducting a survey
6 **Where do bright ideas come from?**	**The Scientific Method:** analyze data, ask a question, do an experiment, do research, draw conclusions, write a hypothesis **Adjectives and Prepositions:** busy with, excited about, good at, interested in, nervous about, worried about	Past simple	**Listening:** Anticipating information **Writing:** Researching and writing a biography **Project:** Preparing for a trip to Mars
7 **When is the right time?**	**Weather:** cloud, cloudy, fog, foggy, rain, rainy, snow, snowy, storm, stormy, sun, sunny, wind, windy	Future: *will*; Future: *going to* Short answers	**Reading:** Previewing to predict content **Speaking:** Storytelling **Project:** Making a poster
8 **How do you feel?**	**Feelings:** anger, angry, embarrassment, embarrassed, excitement, excited, fear, frightened, happiness, happy, jealousy, jealous, sadness, sad, worry, worried	Questions; *What* and *Which*	**Writing:** Expressing opinions in a review essay **Speaking:** Discussing movie reviews **Project:** Making a brochure

Unit 0

1 Unscramble and answer the questions.

0

1

2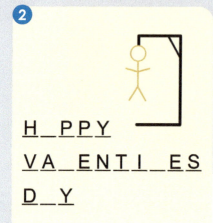

H_PPY
VA_ENTI_ES
D_Y

good at / you / Are / Sudoku puzzles?
<u>Are you good at Sudoku puzzles?</u>
<u>Yes, I am.</u>

Do / jigsaw puzzles? / like / to do / you
_____
_____

Can / in Hangman? / you / spell / words
_____
_____

3

4

you / Can / Rubik's Cube? / the / do
_____
_____

logical order? / Do / see / the / you
_____
_____

2 Write the missing vowels.

House/Apartment	School	Food	Clothes
b <u>e</u> dr <u>o</u> <u>o</u> m	n__t__b__ _k	s__ndw__ch	sw__ __t__r
k__tch__n	t__ __ch__r	w__t__r	sk__rt
ch__ __r	__ngl__sh	p__zz__	j__ __ns

3 Think Fast! Name all the colors in the Rubik's Cube.

4 Make the sentences true for you with *can* or *can't*.

0. I ___can___ whistle my favorite song.
1. My teacher _____ speak Japanese.
2. My best friend _____ play the drums.

3. My parents _____ do a handstand.
4. I _____ sew a button.

5 Look, circle and complete the sentences with numbers.

0. There **is** / **are** ___one___ island in the picture with a very big waterslide on it.
1. There **is** / **are** _____ children in the picture.
2. There **is** / **are** _____ children are in the water.
3. On the slide, there **is** / **are** _____ boys and _____ girls.
4. There **is** / **are** _____ children with sunglasses.
5. There **is** / **are** _____ boy with a hat.

6 Match the numbers and letters on the waterslide.

1. _c_   3. ____   5. ____
2. ____   4. ____

Stop and Think! Can puzzles and challenges help you learn?

7 Complete the questions with *are*, *is* or *there*. Then answer.

1. What color ___are___ the walls in your parents' bedroom? _____
2. What color _____ the door of your bedroom? _____
3. How many windows _____ _____ in your living room? _____
4. How many chairs _____ _____ in the dining room? _____

8 Look and complete the corresponding lines in the text balloons.

I run, I play soccer and I do tae-kwon-do.
☐ I play to win. I'm the champion!

I love swimming and I sometimes win.
☐ But winning is not important for me.

9 How do you play sports? Mark (✓) the opinion you agree with.

10 Read and circle the correct options.

Athletics

Be a Good Athlete!

Sports make you a healthy boy or girl. Follow this advice!

0. **(Practice)** / **Don't practice** every week.
1. **Respect** / **Don't respect** the other players.
2. **Get** / **Don't get** angry when you don't win.
3. **Eat** / **Don't eat** good food: salads, pasta and tuna fish.
4. **Drink** / **Don't drink** a lot of water to be hydrated.
5. **Go** / **Don't go** to bed late.
6. **Keep** / **Don't keep** your uniform clean.

11 **Look at the pictures in the article. Can you see hidden messages?**

Challenges for Our Eyes

We have two eyes in the front of our head. Our eyes can see in color. Can you see numbers in picture 1? That means that your eyes are seeing the colors correctly.

Our eyes and brain give us the ability to see distances between objects (3-D vision). This ability can also make us see things that are not really there. For example, picture 2 is called a stereogram. Can you read the secret message?

But sometimes the eyes and brain don't function 100%. Maybe you can't see in color or you can't see in 3-D. Some people see red and green as the same color and they have difficulty choosing clothes. Some people walk into objects because they can't see the distance correctly. And some people just need glasses to read or see in the distance. Life can be complicated when you don't see well!

If you have vision problems, an optometrist can help you.

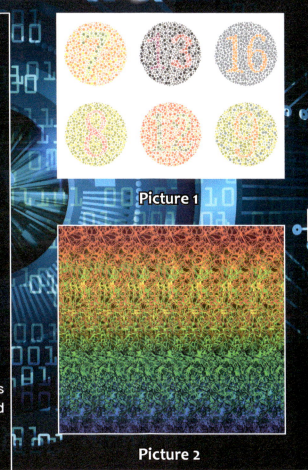

Picture 1

Picture 2

12 **Read the article and mark (✓) the main idea.**
1. ☐ You can test if your eyes work correctly. Maybe you need glasses.
2. ☐ Human eyes are incredible, but some people's eyes are not perfect.
3. ☐ Everybody can see 3-D images. You just need to practice.

13 **Match the visual problems with the pictures.**
1. ☐ a person who can't see colors
2. ☐ a person who can't see in 3-D
3. ☐ a person who needs glasses

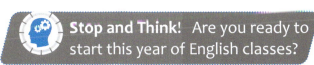
Stop and Think! Are you ready to start this year of English classes?

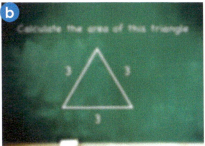

14 🎧¹ **Listen and check your answers.**

Vocabulary

1 Look at the lockers and complete the sentences.

math   music   physical education (P.E.)   Spanish

1. I have a ruler and a calculator because I have _____ today.
2. I have my sneakers and my gym uniform because I have _____ today.
3. I have my recorder in my locker because I have _____ this morning.
4. I have my dictionary today because I have _____.

2 Think Fast! Interview your classmate and mark (✓) the items.

☐ a calculator   ☐ a gym uniform   ☐ a recorder
☐ a dictionary   ☐ sneakers   ☐ a ruler

3 🎧² **Listen and unscramble the school subjects in the pictures.**

1. _____ 2. _____ 3. _____

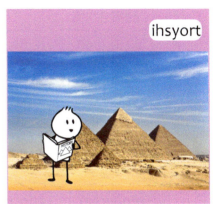

4. _____ 5. _____ 6. _____

4 🎧³ **Listen and circle the correct option.**

1. Today, Pete has math and **chemistry / geography** in the morning.
2. Pete has music and **art / English** in the afternoon.
3. He does his **history / technology** homework in the evening.

5 **Read and match.**

1. ☐ in the evening
2. ☐ in the morning
3. ☐ at night
4. ☐ in the afternoon

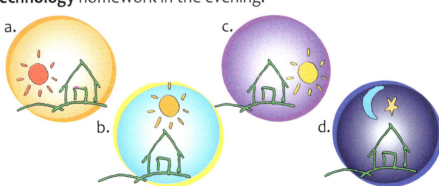

a. c. b. d.

6 **Read and complete the sentences about you.**

1. Today, I have _____ in the morning.
2. Today, I have _____ in the afternoon.
3. I do my _____ homework in the evening.
4. I _____ at night before I go to bed.

Grammar

Eagle Hill Middle School					Grade 6
Hours	Monday	Tuesday	Wednesday	Thursday	Friday
8:30-8:50	Homeroom				
9:00-9:50	Math	Math	(1) _____	Math	Math
10:00-10:50	English	English	(2) _____	English	English
11:00-11:50	Social Studies	Art	(3) _____	Art	Social Studies
12:00-12:50	Lunch Recess				
1:00-1:50	Science	Health	(4) _____	Science	Health
2:00-2:50	Geography	Reading	(5) _____	Spanish	Band
3:00-3:50	Home Economics	Spanish	(6) _____	Home Economics	P.E.

1 🎧⁴ **Listen and complete the class schedule for Wednesday.**

2 🎧⁴ **Listen again and choose the correct option.**
1. We **always** have math at 9 in the **afternoon** / **morning**.
2. We **sometimes** have band practice in the **afternoon** / **evening**.
3. I **usually** eat there, but on **Fridays** / **Wednesdays**, I bring my own lunch.
4. We **never** have reading on Wednesday. It's only on **Tuesday** / **Thursday**.
5. We **often** play soccer in **December** / **September**.

Prepositions

To talk about time, we use
in + *the morning, the afternoon, the evening.*
(But at + *night*)
on + *Monday, Tuesday,* etc.
in + *March, June,* etc.

3 Look and complete the chart.

always
never
often
sometimes
usually

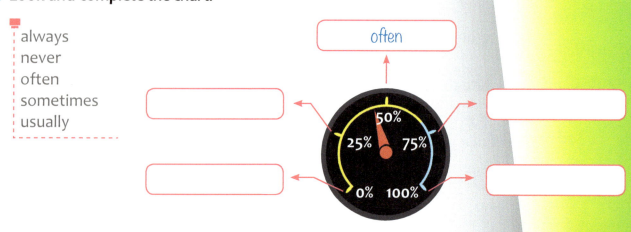

4 Look and answer the quiz.

Do exams make you nervous?

Do you have good exam strategies? Take the quiz and find out.

1 **You need** a good grade on the final. Do you plan your study schedule?
- ☐ Of course! I always plan.
- ☐ I sometimes do.
- ☐ No, **it doesn't help** me.

2 **Does noise distract** you when you study?
- ☐ **Yes, it does.** I need peace and quiet.
- ☐ Music makes studying easier.
- ☐ **No, it doesn't.** It's OK.

3 You have many exams. Do you sleep well the night before them?
- ☐ Yes. I go to bed early.
- ☐ Actually, I like to play video games until late.
- ☐ **No, I don't.** I always feel very nervous.

4 **We don't want** to dehydrate. Do you drink enough water on the day of the exam?
- ☐ Definitely. **It helps** me feel alert.
- ☐ **I don't drink** anything.
- ☐ No, I don't like water.

5 **Do you have** a system to answer the exam questions?
- ☐ The easy questions go first, then the difficult ones.
- ☐ I guess the answers.
- ☐ **I answer** each question one by one.

Mostly red	Excellent! Exams are easy for you.
Mostly blue	You can do better. Change some bad habits.
Mostly green	Help! You need new strategies.

Present Simple

Affirmative
I answer.
It helps.

Negative
I **don't** drink.
It **doesn't** help.

Interrogative
Do you have...?
Does noise **distract** you?

5 Change the sentences to affirmative (+), negative (–) or interrogative (?).

1. Do you have exams every week? (+)
   _____

2. We play basketball in the park. (–)
   _____

3. She studies at night. (–)
   _____

4. Does Tim read novels? (+)
   _____

5. Joe and Lisa go to the movies on Fridays. (?)
   _____

6. Ray doesn't like pizza. (?)
   _____

Listening & Writing

Be Strategic!
When you listen, don't write down every word. Only write down key words like nouns or verbs.

1 🎧⁵ **Listen and answer the questions.**
1. Where do the people in the pictures live?
2. Why do people do this?
3. How old are the people in the pictures?

2 Listen again and circle T (True) or F (False).

1. The **journey** to school in Los Pinos is difficult and exciting.	T	F
2. About five children go to school on the zip line.	T	F
3. The children have a school and a teacher in their **village**.	T	F
4. The children travel on the zip line with a classmate.	T	F
5. The zip line is 800 meters high.	T	F
6. José travels on the zip line.	T	F

18

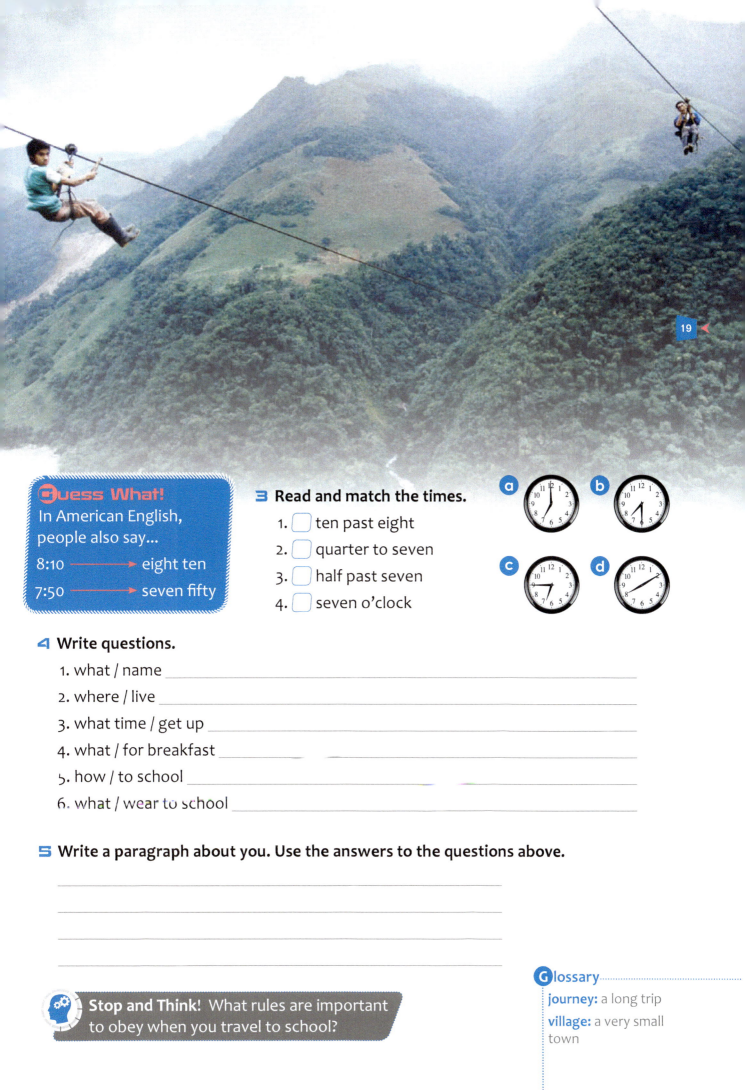

Guess What!
In American English, people also say…
8:10 → eight ten
7:50 → seven fifty

3 Read and match the times.
1. ☐ ten past eight
2. ☐ quarter to seven
3. ☐ half past seven
4. ☐ seven o'clock

a b c d

4 Write questions.
1. what / name _____
2. where / live _____
3. what time / get up _____
4. what / for breakfast _____
5. how / to school _____
6. what / wear to school _____

5 Write a paragraph about you. Use the answers to the questions above.

_____
_____
_____
_____

Stop and Think! What rules are important to obey when you travel to school?

Glossary
journey: a long trip
village: a very small town

Culture

1 Look at the map and circle *T* (True) or *F* (False). Correct the false information.

1. There is only one island in Japan.   T   F
2. Japan is in the Atlantic Ocean.   T   F
3. Japan is a country in Asia.   T   F
4. Japan's flag is red and white.   T   F

2 Complete the interview with these questions.

a. is Japan a clean country?
b. do you think that's a good idea?
c. What school do you go to, Masako?
d. Do you have rules at school?
e. do you wear school uniforms?

Kids Around the World... Japan

Joyce Rice

Hello readers! You probably think schools are the same all over the world, but you are in for a surprise! Meet Masako Shimizu, a twelve-year old girl from Osaka.

Joyce: Masako, thank you for talking to us.

Masako: My pleasure.

J: (1) ☐

M: I go to a junior high school here in Osaka, Japan. My brother goes to the same school because both boys and girls study here. I'm 12 so I'm in grade 1.

J: And tell us, (2) ☐

M: Yes, we do. We call it *seifuku*. The boys wear a black jacket and pants. Girls wear a uniform. They're traditional in Japan.

J: (3) ☐

M: Oh, yes. A lot! For example, we have cleaning period after school every day. We clean every part of the school, including the bathrooms! All Japanese kids do it. It's very common.

J: Amazing! But (4) ☐

M: Yes, I do. It's a very important lesson. We do it because we respect each other. I want my classroom and my school to look nice, but I don't like cleaning the bathrooms very much. That's gross! However, I do it twice a year.

J: And finally, (5) ☐

M: Yes, it is. We don't litter and we don't do graffiti. The trains and buses look new because people don't damage them or make them dirty. We learn to keep our schools and our country neat.

J: Fantastic. Thank you for your help, Masako.

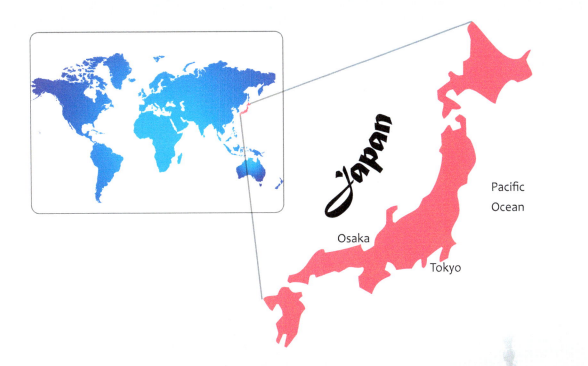

3 **Look at the interview and complete the mind map.**

A Clean Country   Cleaning the School
Introduction   School Uniforms   Value

Kids Around the World: Japan

_____ Part 1

_____ Part 2

_____ Part 3

_____ Part 4

_____ Part 5

 Stop and Think! What are the benefits of having rules at school?

Glossary

junior high school: another name for middle school

gross: horrible

graffiti: drawings or paintings on walls

neat: clean

Project

1. Read the infographic and draw the missing pictures.
2. Review the infographic. Circle two similarities and two differences in your school.
3. Make a list of rules in your school.
4. Create an infographic about your school and present it to the class.

How to Survive Middle School in the U.S.

1. Remember, school starts at 8:30 every day.
- Be on time!
- Don't run in the halls.

22

2. Most kids come to school on the school bus.
- Stay seated during the trip.
- Don't push other students.

3. There are some general rules:
- Don't use phones in class.
- Don't chew gum at school.

4. Some students have lunch in the cafeteria.
- Eat slowly.
- Keep your table clean.

5. All lockers have a combination **padlock**.
- Keep your locker closed.

6. It's important to have everything you need for school.
- Check your backpack before you leave home.
- Don't forget your gym uniform or your rulers.

7. There are many important things to remember at school.
- Use a pinboard app.
- Use **reminders** in your phone.

8. There are many new subjects in middle school. like **foreign** languages or algebra.
- Participate in class.
- Ask questions.

Glossary

padlock: a metal object used to secure doors

reminder: a note to remember something

foreign: belonging to a different country

23

1 Look and complete the crossword with school equipment.

Across → 2. 3. 4. 5.

Down ↓ 1. 3.

2 Read and complete with school subjects.

1. We have _____ today. I love soccer!
2. a²+b² = c²! Gulp! I don't understand _____.
3. We write computer games in our _____ class. It's great!
4. Why are these dates important? 1492? 1789? 1945? I'm terrible at _____.
5. We have a _____ test tomorrow. What's the capital of Ecuador?
6. The _____ laboratory is a dangerous place. We use acid in our lessons.

3 Circle the correct option.

1. We catch the school bus early **in / at / on** the morning.
2. I play computer games **in / at / on** night.
3. Band practice is **in / at / on** Friday.
4. My birthday is **in / at / on** June.

4 Complete the sentences using the words in parentheses.

1. I forget my gym uniform. (*never*)
   _____

2. We eat lunch at school. (*sometimes*)
   _____

3. Our teacher gives us homework. (*often*)
   _____

4. I watch TV after school. (*usually*)
   _____

5. Does Kim sit next to you? (*always*)
   _____

5 Read and complete the sentences.

1. Nigel _____ (+, *play*) hockey.
2. My brother _____ (–, *have*) school tomorrow.
3. The bus _____ (+, *leave*) at 5 o'clock.
4. My mom _____ (+, *watch*) TV every night.
5. My dad _____ (–, *play*) soccer.
6. Rachel _____ (–, *eat*) at the school cafeteria.

6 Look and unscramble the questions. Then write short answers.

JFK Middle School? / she / go / to / does

_____
_____

today? / we / do / chemistry / have

_____
_____

they / English? / do / speak

_____
_____

you / in the afternoon? / play / do / basketball

_____
_____

Just for Fun

1 Unscramble the words. Then decode the message.

HATM ⬜⬜⬜⬜
　　　　13

MUISC ⬜⬜⬜⬜⬜
　　　10　4　11

NIPHASS ⬜⬜⬜⬜⬜⬜⬜
　　　　1　　16

ATLERTERUI ⬜⬜⬜⬜⬜⬜⬜⬜⬜⬜
　　　　　8　5

REGPYHGOA ⬜⬜⬜⬜⬜⬜⬜⬜⬜
　　　　　　　　7

MIEHRSTCY ⬜⬜⬜⬜⬜⬜⬜⬜⬜
　　　　6　9　14

TAR ⬜⬜⬜
　　12

TONCEHLYGO ⬜⬜⬜⬜⬜⬜⬜⬜⬜⬜
　　　　2

RTHOISY ⬜⬜⬜⬜⬜⬜⬜
　　　　15　3

My favorite subject:

⬜⬜⬜⬜⬜⬜⬜⬜　　D⬜⬜⬜⬜⬜⬜⬜
1　2　3　4　5　6　7　8　　9　10　11　12　13　14　15　16

2 Look and match.

 hav
 make
 sle
 hel
 ea
 stud

 ies
 ps
 e
 ts
 ep
 s

3 Look and guess. Is it…
1. ⬜ a table leg?
2. ⬜ a recorder?
3. ⬜ a pen?

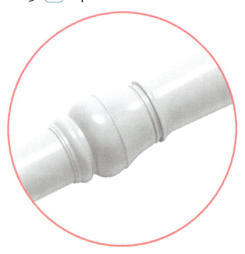

4 Answer the riddle.

What always runs but never walks, often murmurs but never talks, has a bed but never sleeps, has a mouth but never eats ?

What's the best job?

2

Vocabulary

1 Look and write the people's names.

| Get to Know the Center | Admissions | Research | News and Events |

Overview
Visit
Contact us

Learn about the People and their Professions

There are many professions in the world today. People choose their future careers based on their likes and dislikes and their strengths and weaknesses. Here are some examples of people who love what they do.

- My name's Joanna and I'm an engineer. I love mathematics. I work in an automobile factory. We use robots to assemble the cars. I design the plans to build those robots.

- Hi. I'm Sheila and I work as a pilot for a commercial airline. I like traveling to different countries and meeting people. My job is to fly passengers to different parts of the world. I love that!

- I'm Roy and I work at the fire station. I'm a firefighter. My job is to put out fires and help people in dangerous situations. I love helping others.

- I'm Emma and I work as a transit operator. I drive a train every day from 9 to 5. I enjoy this job a lot. I love helping people move around our city.

- My name's Richard and I work at a hotel downtown. I work as a receptionist at the front desk. I welcome guests and help them with their rooms. It's a very busy job, but I love interacting with people.

- I'm Paul and I work in a salon in a shopping mall in the suburbs. I'm a hairstylist. In my job I meet a lot of people. I help them look good with a trendy haircut or a new hairstyle. I need to learn new techniques all the time.

2 **Think Fast!** Circle the professions in the text.

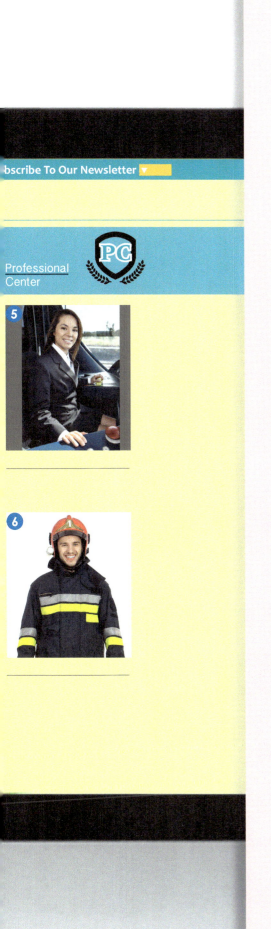

3 **Unscramble the professions. Then match them to their workplaces.**

1. ☐ neregine _____
2. ☐ rihieegffrt _____
3. ☐ airhistylts _____
4. ☐ ploit _____
5. ☐ seeinrtpicot _____
6. ☐ sartnti rtporeoa _____

a. factory   b. airport   c. fire station

d. train station   e. hotel   f. salon

4 **Read and identify the professions.**

1. A _____ moves people around the city and works from 9 to 5.
2. A _____ flies passengers to different places around the world.
3. A _____ helps people look good with a new haircut or hairstyle.
4. A _____ helps put out fires and helps people in danger.
5. A _____ welcomes guests and provides help regarding their rooms.
6. An _____ designs plans to build robots in car factories.

 Stop and Think! What is most important in a job?

Grammar

1 Read the chats and identify where Jo's friends are.

home

the gym

a farm

 30

a

Tom: Look:

Jo: What are they doing? Dancing?

Tom: No, they're not dancing. They're taking a pilates class.

b

Nicole: Look!

Jo: Are you having cupcakes now?

Nicole: No, I'm not. My mom's baking them at home. These are the first. We need 40 for the school drama festival.

c

Jerry:

Jo: Wow, what's that?

Jerry: That's Lolly, the cow. I'm helping my grandpa mil the cows this morning.

2 **Read the chats and choose the correct option.**
1. When is Tom taking a pilates class?   a) now   b) every day
2. When is Jerry helping his grandpa?   a) every morning   b) this morning
3. When is Nicole baking cupcakes?   a) at this moment   b) all week

Present Continuous

Jo **is eating** a hot dog.
(be) (-ing)

3 **Look and match.**
1. ☐ I'm doing   a. doing?
2. ☐ He's not taking   b. playing soccer.
3. ☐ Are they going   c. dad in the garden.
4. ☐ What are you   d. my homework.
5. ☐ She's helping her   e. a music class.
6. ☐ We're not   f. to the concert?

4 🎧⁶ **Listen and match. Which speaker is…**

② ☐ in New York?

③ ☐ at school?

① ☐ on a bus?

Prepositions

on + public transportation
at + buildings
in + geographical areas
But *in* for cars and taxis.

5 **Read and complete the sentences.**
1. We're playing volleyball **at / on** the gym today.
2. They're going home **in / on** the train.
3. It's raining **in / at** San Francisco.
4. We're going to the movies **in / on** a taxi.
5. I'm waiting **at / on** the supermarket.
6. She's traveling to Bogotá **at / on** a plane.

Reading & Writing

1 Look at the pictures and the title of the article. What do you think it is about?

Strange Jobs

Are you feeling hungry?

By Claire Rhine

> 32

I'm in a TV studio. In front of me, there is a plate of **grubs**. Sharon Majkowski, 26, is slowly eating them. It's not her lunch. This is her job. Sharon is a **stunt** tester.

When you watch a reality TV show, you often see people do **challenges**.

For example, they might live in the jungle without bedrooms, bathrooms or even eat disgusting food!

A stunt tester does all the challenges before the TV show. If a challenge is risky, Sharon discovers it first!

> **A stunt tester does all the challenges before the TV show.**

"Sometimes they ask me to eat live animals,"

she says. "I always refuse because it's cruel. I eat anything if it's dead. These cooked grubs are good, actually. Do you want one?"

Politely, we **refuse**. They look revolting. This one is clearly a job for the experts.

2 Read the article and circle *T* (True) or *F* (False).

1. Sharon appears on TV.   T   F
2. A stunt tester tries the challenges before the show.   T   F
3. Sharon only eats live animals.   T   F
4. Sharon thinks cooked grubs are delicious.   T   F

Be Strategic!
In a text, there are **facts**, information that can be verified, and **opinions**, personal beliefs about something or someone.

3 Find two facts and two opinions in the article. Write them in your notebook.

4 Read the e-mail and number the sections.

1. **Closing.** Use "Regards" (Best / Sincerely) and a comma. Then write your name.
2. **Greeting.** Use "Dear," the person's name and a comma.
3. **Body of the message.** One paragraph per idea. Check your spelling and grammar!

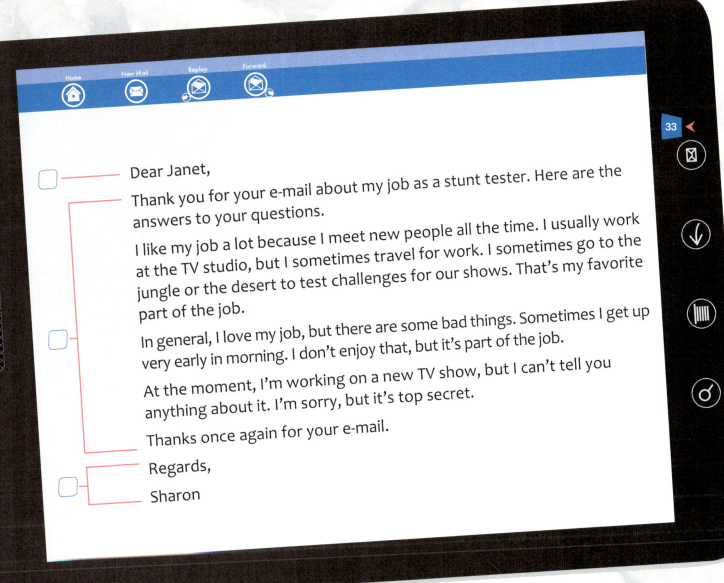

Dear Janet,

Thank you for your e-mail about my job as a stunt tester. Here are the answers to your questions.

I like my job a lot because I meet new people all the time. I usually work at the TV studio, but I sometimes travel for work. I sometimes go to the jungle or the desert to test challenges for our shows. That's my favorite part of the job.

In general, I love my job, but there are some bad things. Sometimes I get up very early in morning. I don't enjoy that, but it's part of the job.

At the moment, I'm working on a new TV show, but I can't tell you anything about it. I'm sorry, but it's top secret.

Thanks once again for your e-mail.

Regards,
Sharon

5 Write an e-mail about an imaginary job you have. Explain:

1. What you do
2. What you like
3. What you don't like
4. What you're doing now

Stop and Think! Can a job be dangerous? Is it OK?

Glossary

grub: a baby insect like a worm

stunt: a dangerous action done by someone in a film

challenge: a difficult action to test someone's ability

refuse: to say no to something

Podcasts Live

> 34

Hi, I'm Joanne. Today on *Podcasts Live*, I'm visiting a company with a difference. Can you guess what it is? Here are some clues. The company (1) _____ in the technology sector. It's very, very (2) _____ and you probably use it several times a day. I'm in their offices now in California, in the U.S. It is a very unusual company. Listen to these examples: A woman is (3) _____ her dog at the office! A man is (4) _____ coffee in the corridors. Two women are **sunbathing** on a balcony. Some people are (5) _____ yoga, in the office! One person is (6) _____ on the wall! I mean, is anybody working here? Where am I?

1 Read and mark (✓) the pictures mentioned in the podcast.

2 🎧⁷ Listen and complete.

3 🎧⁸ Read again and guess the company. Listen and check.

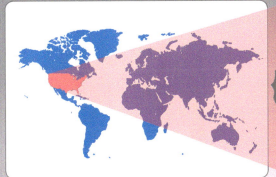

Business, U.S.

Many big technology companies like Google have their **headquarters** in Silicon Valley in California. Businesspeople do important and challenging work there, but life there can also be relaxed. For instance, **employees** at Google wear casual clothes, play games and do fun activities during work hours. Why? Google knows innovation and collaboration are important. To make this happen, the company provides employees with everything they need to feel happy. Google workers have access to free food, rest areas, medical attention and recreational spaces. What's the idea behind all of these **perks**? The company believes that when people are relaxed and comfortable or are having fun, they are more creative. Google encourages employees to solve problems using their own solutions, not their managers'. With a comfortable work environment and good social relationships, teams make big impacts. Not every company is like Google, but it is a pioneer in innovation and flexibility for many modern companies throughout the world to follow.

 Stop and Think! What does it mean to feel happy with a job?

4 Read and circle *T* (True) or *F* (False).

1. The company is in Nevada, in Silicon Valley.   T   F
2. Workers wear suits.   T   F
3. Workers don't have any perks.   T   F
4. Google welcomes original ideas.   T   F
5. Google is a traditional company.   T   F

Glossary

sunbathe: stay in the sun to make your skin brown

headquarters: the main office of a large company

employees: people who work for a company

perks: benefits given in a job

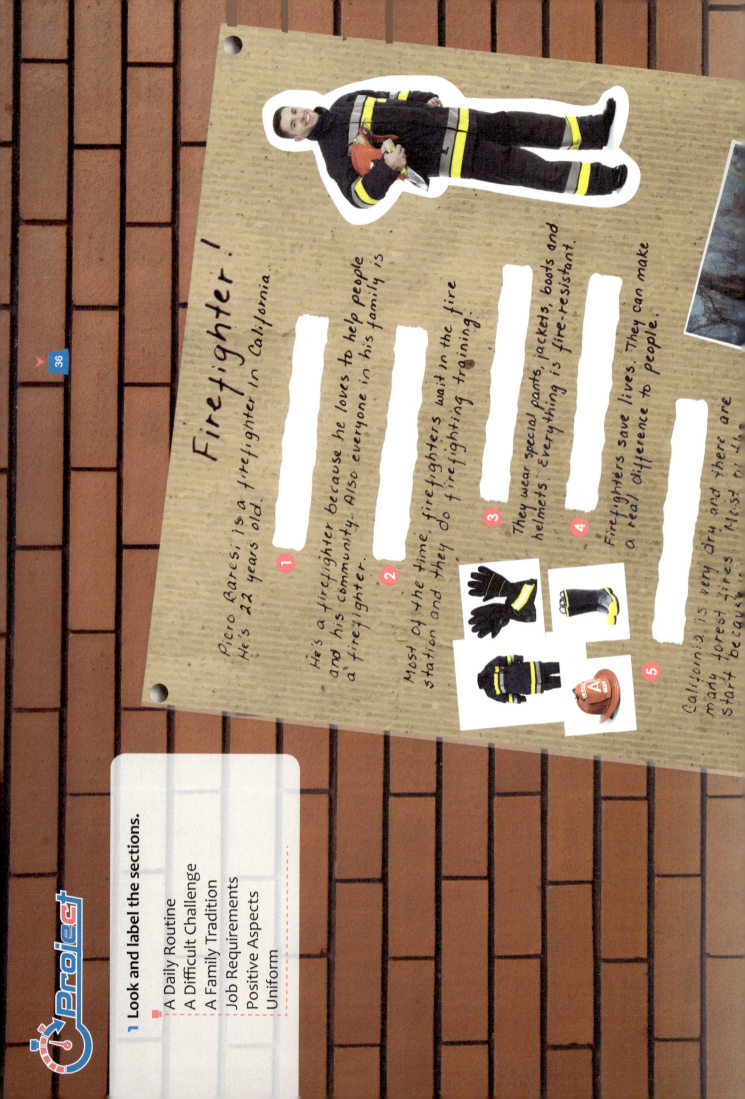

In California, firefighters must be over 18. They need a high school diploma and they need to be physically fit.

Today, Piero is taking a driving test so he can drive the fire engine. He's waiting for the driver instructor. Piero isn't worried. As a firefighter, he is prepared for anything!

2 Read and match the sentence fragments.

1. ☐ Everyone in Piero's family is
2. ☐ At the station, firefighters
3. ☐ A firefighter's equipment is
4. ☐ Weather conditions in California
5. ☐ People's bad
6. ☐ Firefighters need to show

a. a firefighter.
b. contribute to forest fires.
c. decisions can cause a fire.
d. fire-resistant.
e. learn what to do in a fire situation.
f. proof of their age, education and physical fitness.

3 Write about your dream job. Do research on the following topics.

- why this job is important
- special clothes / uniform to wear
- some good aspects about the job
- something challenging about the job
- any training or requirements needed for the job

4 Make a poster about your dream job. Present it to the class.

- Find photos you can use.
- Plan a design for your poster.
- Write the text for every section. Use the model poster as a guide.
- Check your grammar and punctuation.

37

Review

1 Read and match.

1. ◯ A firefighter
2. ◯ A hairstylist
3. ◯ A pilot
4. ◯ A receptionist
5. ◯ A transit operator
6. ◯ An engineer

a. designs and builds machines.
b. welcomes and helps guests with their stays.
c. helps people in dangerous situations.
d. moves people in a city.
e. flies passengers to different destinations.
f. gives people new looks.

2 Unscramble the words.

oparrti
_____

atfryco
_____

ifer nitatso
_____

etlho
_____

nsalo
_____

antir nosiatt
_____

3 Look and write sentences. What are they doing?

_____

_____

_____

_____

4 Correct the sentences.
1. I sitting on the bus. _____
2. What are you do? _____
3. We not doing homework. _____
4. Are you have lunch at school today? _____
5. Jim is no playing basketball. _____
6. Are you watch TV? _____

5 Answer the questions about you.
1. Are you having P.E. today?
_____
2. What are your parents doing right now?
_____
3. What are you doing right now?
_____
4. Are you reading a book at the moment?
_____
5. Who is sitting in front of/behind you today?
_____
6. Is your teacher wearing a sweater today?
_____

6 Write the correct preposition.
at in on

1. _____ Canon City, Colorado
2. _____ the restaurant
3. _____ the bookstore
4. _____ the electronics store
5. _____ a taxi
6. _____ the bus

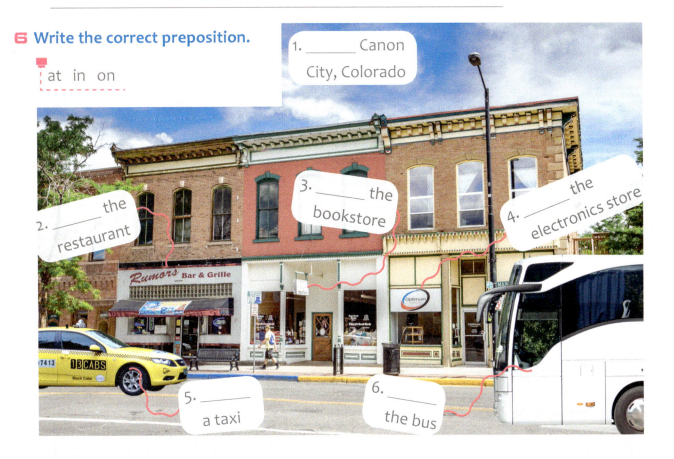

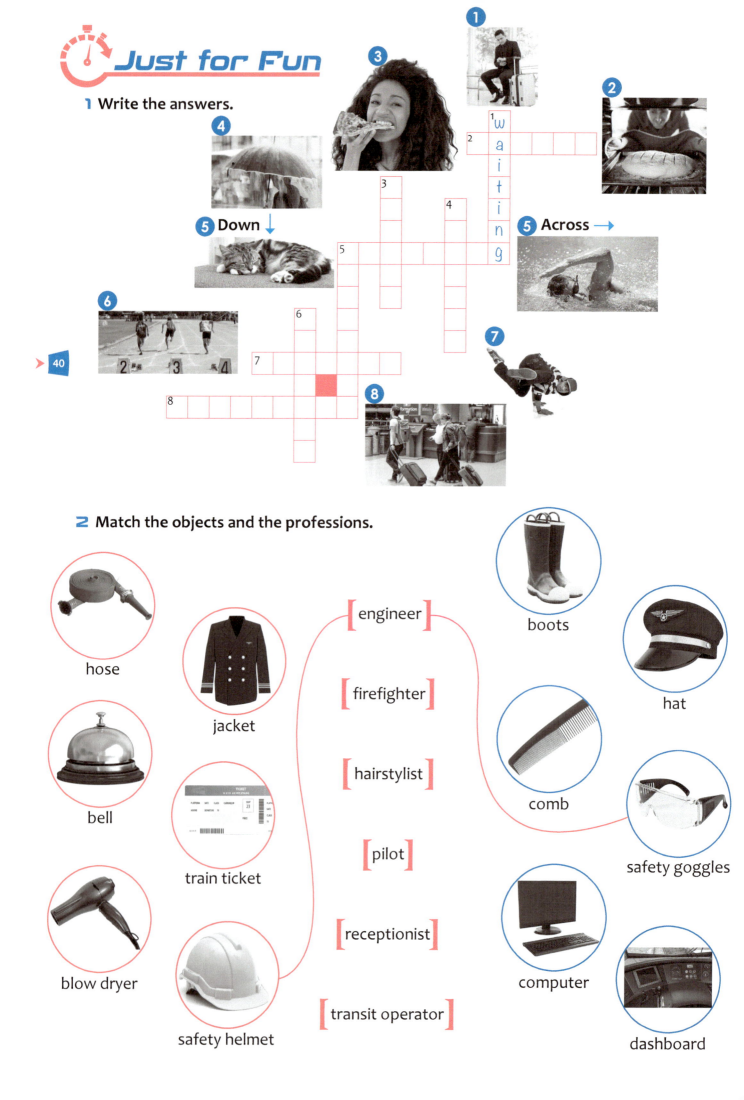

Vocabulary

1 🎧⁹ Listen and circle the correct option.

CLEARANCE
SELLING BLOWOUT

1. hat / blouse
2. sneakers / T-shirt
3. jeans / dress
4. shorts / coat
5. scarf / jeans
6. sweater / skirt
7. hat / dress
8. dress / shorts
9. pants / socks
10. sneakers / shorts
11. dress / sweater
12. pants / socks

Guess What!
You don't always need a dictionary to find new words. For clothing, look at websites like www.macys.com

42

Belts

Costume Jewelry

EXTRA 20% OFF
EXTRA 15% OR 10% OFF
Home & select depts. Excludes specials

2 Think Fast! What other clothes words do you know? Make a list.

3 🎧¹⁰ Listen and write the clothes each person mentions.

Lisa _____
Ruth _____
Billy _____
Alberto _____

4 🎧¹⁰ Listen again and match the speakers to the problems.

1. Lisa   a. makes mistakes doing laundry.
2. Ruth   b. can't find clothes that fit.
3. Billy   c. lives far from the clothing stores.
4. Alberto   d. can't find shoes his size.

5 Look and identify the events. What clothes can you wear for them?

① Crash the Party!
Fran's 14th birthday
Friday, February 10th
17320 NE Sacramento Street
Portland, Oregon
555-756-6432

② Hey, do you want to go to a movie premiere this afternoon? 13:36
Sure, what is it? 13:38
The new dinosaur movie. 13:42
👎👎 13:45

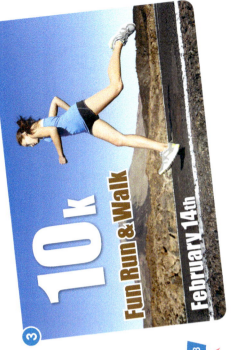

③ 10k Fun Run & Walk
February 14th

43

1 🎧¹¹ **Read the comic and complete the sentences. Then listen and check.**

cheaper   larger   more expensive   more polite   smaller

1. The chicken mask is _____ **than** the dog mask.
2. The dog mask is _____ **than** the chicken mask.
3. The stormtrooper helmet is _____ **than** the robot mask.
4. The robot mask is _____ **than** the stormtrooper helmet.
5. The woman is _____ **than** the man.

Comparatives

small — small**er**

expensive — **more** expensive

Note: heavy → heavier
large → larger

2 **Look and write the comparatives.**

1. fast _____
2. old _____
3. funny _____
4. serious _____
5. short _____
6. modern _____
7. long _____
8. late _____

CAN I HELP YOU?

There's a costume party and contest and I don't know what to wear. I have three good options but I want **the best** one.

The robot is **the cheapest** costume and it's **the easiest** one to make!

The bear costume is **the funniest** but it's very hot and heavy.

I like the stormtrooper armor because I love the *Star Wars* movies. It's **the most expensive** costume because it has **the coolest** accesories!

Please help me choose!

Jo

Superlatives

tall	taller	the tallest
difficult	more difficult	the most difficult

Note: heavy → the heaviest
large → the largest

3 Read the e-mail and complete the questions. Then answer them.

1. Which is _____ _____ costume? (*expensive*)
2. Which is _____? (*funny*)
3. Which costume is _____? (*cheap*)
4. Which costume is _____ option? (*good*)

4 Complete with a comparative or superlative adjective.

1. The robot costume is _____ option. (*practical*)
2. I'm _____ Jo. I need the bear costume. (*tall*)
3. The chicken mask is _____ the dog mask. (*funny*)
4. For me, the dog mask is _____ option! (*cool*)

Reading & Listening

Be Strategic!
Look at a text and its pictures quickly **to get a general idea** of the content (skimming). Read fast and **find specific information** (scanning).

1 Think Fast! What's on the page? How do you know? (1 min)

Starters

Caesar Salad — $12.90
Fresh romaine lettuce and croutons, served with chicken sauteed in butter, salt and pepper

Green Salad — $11.90
Three types of lettuce, tomatoes and sweet corn

Appetizers

Buffalo Wings — $8.50
Chicken wings lightly fried with buffalo sauce and blue cheese dressing

Nachos — $5.50
Tortilla chips with cheese sauce, black olives and guacamole

Main Course

Cod and Rice — $35.50
Grilled cod served with white rice

Strip Steak — $42.00
Half-kilo steak served with baked potato and steamed vegetables

Veggie Cheeseburger — $25.90
Made with beans and served with french fries

Desserts

Fruit Salad — $13.50
Slices of orange, kiwi, banana, melon and apple

Ice Cream — $9.90
Two scoops: vanilla, strawberry or chocolate

Cheesecake — $8.50
Plain or topped with juicy strawberries

Drinks

Coffee (Regular or decaf)	$2.50
Hot Chocolate	$2.75
Hot or Iced Tea	$2.00
Milkshake	$3.00
Sodas	$3.50

2 Scan the menu and answer the questions.

1. Can you get vanilla ice cream?
   _____

2. How much is a milkshake and a piece of cheesecake?
   _____

3. What appetizer is the most expensive?
   _____

4. You want a salad and a drink. What can you get for $14?
   _____

5. Can you get fish for the main course?
   _____

6. How much do you need for the cheapest starter, main course and drink?
   _____

3 🎧12 Listen and circle Paul's choices on the menu.

4 🎧12 Listen again and choose the correct options.

1. Nachos have a lot of **salt** / **sugar**.
2. Doctors say it's OK to eat a little **red** / **white** meat a day.
3. The problem with the burger is the **French fries** / **mayonnaise**.
4. The fruit salad is **better** / **worse** than the ice cream.
5. Sodas are the worst drinks. They contain lots of **salt** / **sugar**.

 Stop and Think! How do you choose what to buy in a restaurant?

Glossary
cod: a large sea fish
veggie: (inf.) vegetarian
slice: a thin cut of meat, vegetables or fruit
scoop: a ball of ice cream

Culture

1 Complete the text with the superlative form of the adjectives.

DID YOU KNOW

China is one of (1) _____ (*old*) civilizations in the world. Many of (2) _____ (*important*) inventions come from there, including **silk** and paper. It is one of (3) _____ (*big*) countries in the world and it has (4) _____ (*large*) population on the planet: around 1.3 billion people! Today it is also one of (5) _____ (*rich*) countries in the world. Businesses in China make most of the things we use every day.

2 Look at the pictures on the cell phone. How are they related?

3 🎧 13 Unscramble the words and complete the sentences. Listen and check.

1. I am happy today. It's my _____ (*yrdbahit*).
2. It's a book about _____ (*asct*). I love them!
3. And my grandparents always give me some _____ (*yenmo*).
4. Do you have a birthday _____ (*kcae*)?

4 🎧 13 Correct the false information. Then listen again to check.

1. In China, we don't get lots of toys.
2. It's a tradition to give a card in a red envelope.
3. I have a cake with 14 **candles** for me this year.
4. This special **noodle** represents happiness.
5. I'm very sad with my birthday **gifts**.

5 Mark (✓) the best summary.

1. ☐ In China, kids always get books and money as birthday gifts.
2. ☐ In China, birthday gifts have a special meaning.

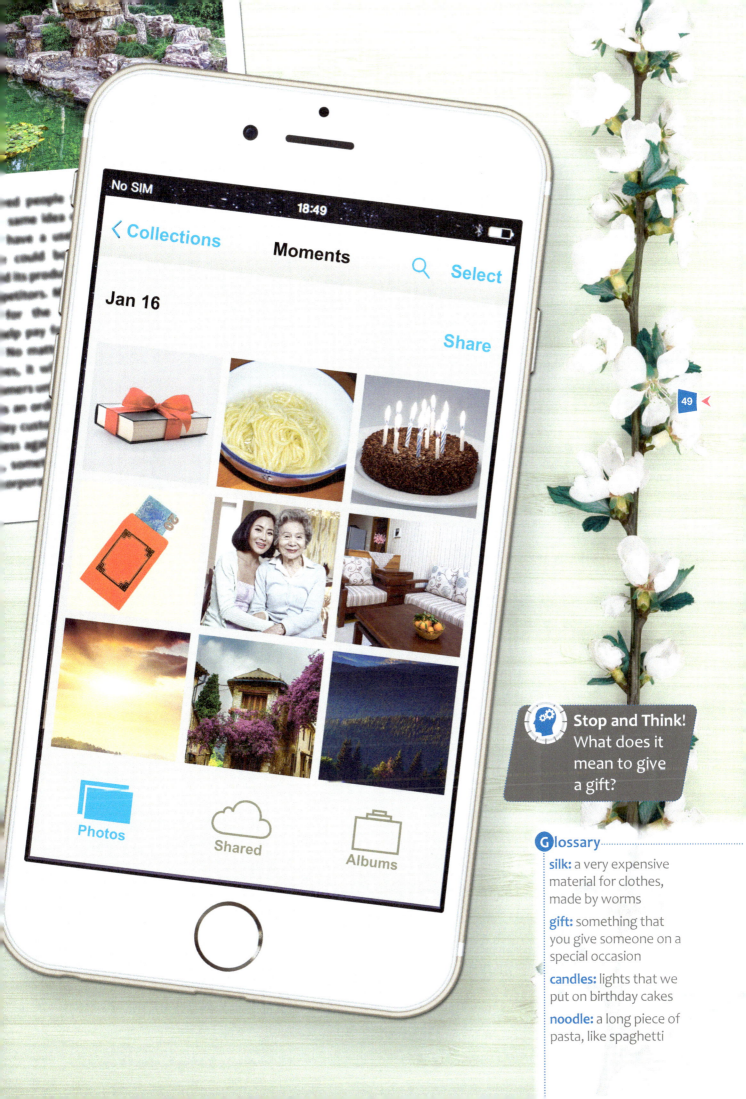

Stop and Think! What does it mean to give a gift?

Glossary

silk: a very expensive material for clothes, made by worms

gift: something that you give someone on a special occasion

candles: lights that we put on birthday cakes

noodle: a long piece of pasta, like spaghetti

# Project

1 Unscramble the sentences. Which are true for you?

1. at home / I / some money. / do jobs / to earn
2. never / I / money! / any / have
3. for emergencies. / some money / save / always / I
4. My parents / me / give / every week. / some money
5. spend / always / I / my money. / all of

2 Write the letters of the tips on the bulletin board.

1. ☐ $10 or $9.99?
2. ☐ Beware of the mess!
3. ☐ Look up, look down.
4. ☐ Rock and shop!
5. ☐ Shop big.
6. ☐ This one's half price!

3 Look at the highlighted words in the board. Choose the correct option.

1. *Hip* in letter **a** means
   a. sad   b. popular   c. angry
2. The word *bargain* in **b** refers to something that is
   a. horrible clothes   b. big   c. economical
3. In **c**, the word *messy* probably means
   a. disorganized   b. colorful   c. delicious
4. The word *cent* in **d** probably refers to
   a. clothes   b. food   c. money
5. In **e**, the word *shelf* means
   a. a basket   b. a bag   c. a board
6. *Shopping carts* in letter **f** refers to
   a. plastic bags   b. mobile baskets   c. big boxes

4 Design your own bulletin board with money-saving tips. Present it to the class.

1. Use your ideas or do research on the Internet.
2. Plan an attractive design.
3. Check your spelling and punctuation.

TOP TIPS WHEN SHOPPING

a Watch for the **hip** music stores play. It makes you feel excited and want to spend money.

b Stores put more expensive clothes next to similar cheaper ones. The cheaper ones look like a **bargain**! Are they really?

c Clothes in **messy** piles are not an accident. People feel curious, walk over and end up buying something!

d One **cent** makes all the difference. People don't notice the cents, only the first number. Watch out for the prices.

e Want to buy some cookies or potato chips? The most expensive ones are always on the middle **shelf** because you see them first. Cheaper products are on the top and bottom shelves.

f Supermarkets have big **shopping carts** so you can put more things in them! Do you really need to buy all that stuff?

Review

1 Find 12 words in the word snake.

T-shirt sneakers hat blouse shorts coat scarf jeans dress sweater pants socks

2 Cross out the word that doesn't belong in each sentence.

1. It's cold, so put on **a scarf** / **some shorts** / **a sweater**.
2. It's hot today, so wear **a coat** / **shorts** / **a T-shirt**.
3. We have P.E this afternoon, so take your **blouse** / **shorts** / **sneakers** to school.
4. This is a formal dinner, so wear **a blouse** / **a dress** / **jeans**.
5. For the 10K race I need new **dresses** / **sneakers** / **shorts**.
6. We don't have a uniform, so boys usually wear a **dress** / **pants** / **jeans** to school.
7. The **coat** / **dress** / **skirt** goes from her neck to her knees.
8. We can't see his face because he's wearing **a hat** / **a scarf** / **sneakers**.

3 Complete with the comparative form of the adjectives.

1. The City Mall is _____ (*modern*) than the Western Mall.
2. My brother is _____ (*serious*) than me.
3. My sister is _____ (*young*) than me.
4. Pedro is _____ (*tall*) than me.
5. My grandpa is _____ (*old*) than my dad.
6. The bear costume is _____ (*funny*) than the pirate costume.
7. A chicken is _____ (*small*) than a bear.
8. Your hair is _____ (*long*) than mine.

4 Write the comparative forms and number the pictures.

1. beautiful _____
2. cheap _____
3. dangerous _____
4. difficult _____
5. slow _____
6. strong _____

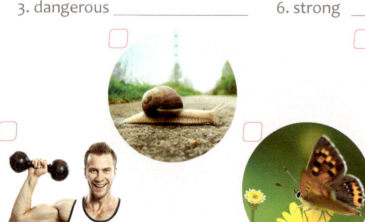

Amazing Facts 65...

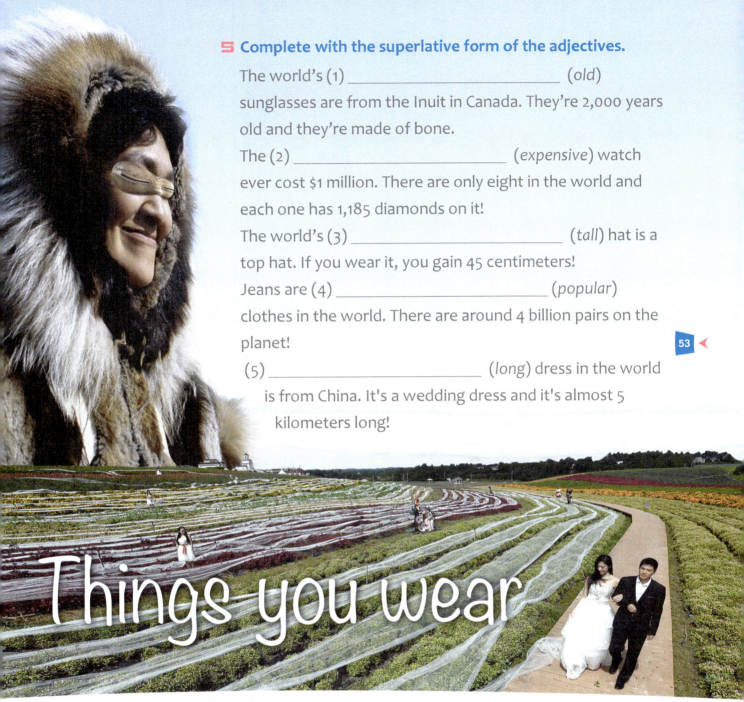

5 Complete with the superlative form of the adjectives.

The world's (1) _____ (old) sunglasses are from the Inuit in Canada. They're 2,000 years old and they're made of bone.

The (2) _____ (expensive) watch ever cost $1 million. There are only eight in the world and each one has 1,185 diamonds on it!

The world's (3) _____ (tall) hat is a top hat. If you wear it, you gain 45 centimeters!

Jeans are (4) _____ (popular) clothes in the world. There are around 4 billion pairs on the planet!

(5) _____ (long) dress in the world is from China. It's a wedding dress and it's almost 5 kilometers long!

Things you wear

6 Choose the correct options to complete the sentences.

1. I called my teacher "mom!" It was the **more embarrassing** / **most embarrassing** moment of my life!
2. This week's homework is **more difficult** / **most difficult** than last week's.
3. I'm **the shortest** / **the shorter** student in my class, but I'm also the **good** / **best** soccer player!
4. The pyramids in Egypt are **the oldest** / **older** than the Golden Gate Bridge.
5. A truck is **heaviest** / **heavier** than a bicycle.
6. Ms. Langley is the **stricter** / **strictest** teacher in the school.
7. People in the countryside are **friendlier** / **friendliest** than people in the city.
8. It's very cold, so wear the **thicker** / **thickest** sweater you have.

Just for Fun

1 Find and mark (✓) two identical images.

2 Solve the riddle.

A group of students is participating in a basketball tournament. After the game they take a shower and get dressed to go home. But their shoes are all mixed! They're all the same color and the only difference is the sizes. They're 6, 7, 8, 9 and 10. Can you help them?
- Sean's shoes are smaller than Tim's.
- Roy says his shoes are larger than Tim's but smaller than Matt's.
- Mike's shoes are larger than Matt's.

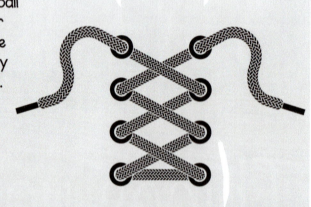

	Sean	Matt	Tim	Mike	Roy
shoe size					

3 Answer the questions.

1. What Internet word is represented by this picture?

_____

HOROBOD

2. What famous name do these letters represent?

_____

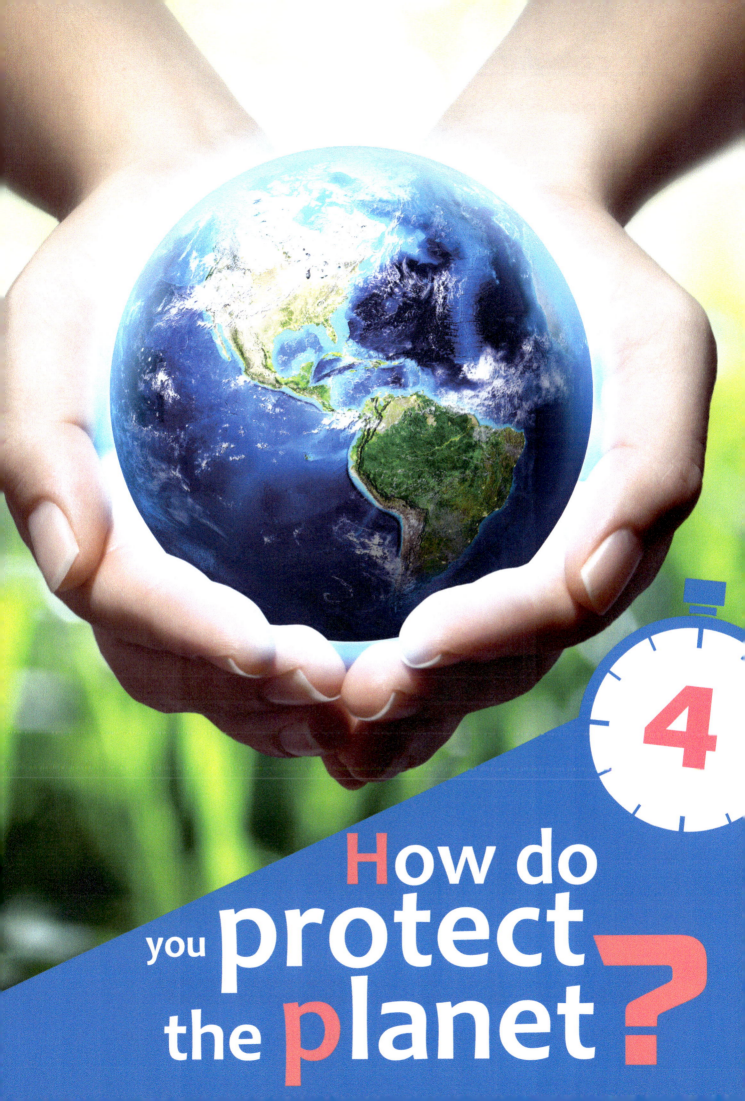

 Vocabulary

1 Read and classify the vegetables and fruits.

Hot Potatoes	
Vegetables	Quantity
1. _____	_____
2. _____	_____
3. _____	_____
4. _____	_____

Go Bananas	
Fruits	Quantity
1. _____	_____
2. _____	_____
3. _____	_____
4. _____	_____

Garden Project
FV Middle School

Welcome to the annual FVMS Garden Project! Like every year, we have a competition to see which team in our school can grow the most food in our own school garden. This year's teams are the *Hot Potatoes* and the *Go Bananas*. The *Hot Potatoes*, led by music teacher Mr. Steele, are growing vegetables. Mr. Steele is working with students from 7th and 8th grade. Ms. Dance, our Spanish teacher, is leading the *Go Bananas* with students from 8th grade. They are growing fruits. We wish everyone the best of luck! Go teams! This year FVMS students are growing:

Florence Valley • Middle School

 2 Think Fast! Can you think of five more fruits and vegetables?

3 🎧¹⁴ Listen and write the quantities in the table. Who won the competition?

4 Match the recommendations using the picture.
1. ☐ Plant seeds in the ground. Potatoes and onions don't grow from seeds.
2. ☐ Put fertilizer on the seeds to help them grow.
3. ☐ Water the ground. Water the plants regularly or they die.
4. ☐ Remove any weeds around your baby plants.
5. ☐ Keep an eye out for caterpillars and snails. They eat fruit and vegetables!
6. ☐ Don't kill the earthworms! They help plants grow.
7. ☐ When you have some fruit, pick it off the tree.
8. ☐ When you have some potatoes, dig them up out of the ground.

5 Cross out the word that doesn't belong in each sentence.
1. Water the **weeds** / **tomatoes** / **tree** once a week.
2. **Caterpillars** / **Earthworms** / **Snails** are eating my plants!
3. **Fertilizers** / **Earthworms** / **Snails** are good for plants.
4. Let's pick some **caterpillars** / **oranges** / **strawberries**.
5. This is a good place to plant **fertilizers** / **onions** / **seeds**.
6. I don't want **caterpillars** / **seeds** / **weeds** in my garden!

Guess What!
If you are very good at gardening, you have a *green thumb*.

Grammar

1 🎧15 Listen and label the objects on the table.

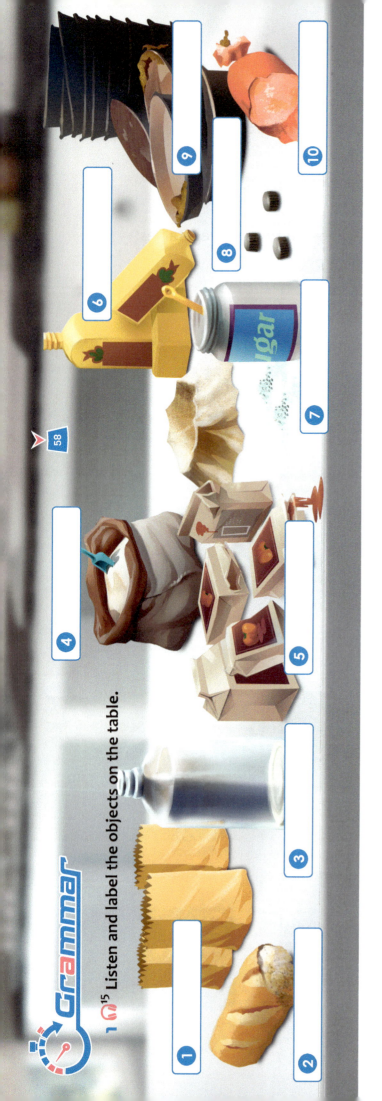

2 Write the words in the correct recycling bin.

Sort Your Garbage and Help the Planet!

mixed | bottles and cans | paper | food

3 Look at the items in Activity 1 and choose the correct option.

1. There's **a lot of** / **a little** salami.
2. How **much** / **little** milk is there?
3. There's **a lot of** / **some** flour.
4. There **isn't any** / **some** salt.
5. There's **a lot of** / **a little** sugar.
6. There **isn't a little** / **any** coffee.

Uncountable nouns

You can't count them!

not any   a little   some   a lot (of)

Note: How much soda...?

4 Look at table again and complete the chart.

Countable nouns

You can count them!

not any   a few   some   a lot (of)

Note: How many cherries...?

5 Unscramble the sentences.

1. milk / the cake. / There's / for / a little
_____
2. is / there? / much / oil / How
_____
3. can see / I / some / in the bag. / flour
_____
4. There are / on / the table. / dishes / a lot of
_____
5. many / How / you have? / do / boxes
_____
6. tomatoes. / aren't / any / There
_____

 Stop and Think! What things do you recycle?

a few _____

some _____

a lot _____

Writing & Speaking

1 Match the descriptions with the paragraphs in the essay.
1. ☐ Conclusion: explain why it is your favorite animal.
2. ☐ Is the animal an endangered species? Is it a popular pet?
3. ☐ Introduction: a description of the animal
4. ☐ The animal's lifestyle: where does it live? What does it eat?

My Favorite Animal: the Chipmunk

a The chipmunk is my favorite animal. It is a mammal with brown, white and black fur. They are very small and they are a lot of fun.

b The chipmunk's habitat is North America. It lives in forests and trees, but it also lives in towns and cities. It mainly eats seeds and nuts.

c Chipmunks are not an endangered species. There are millions of them in North America. They are common, but they are wild animals. People do not keep chipmunks as pets.

d I love chipmunks because they're cute and funny. My family lives in Pennsylvania and we have a lot of chipmunks in our backyard. It's nice to see them in their natural habitat.

Key Words
species (n) – a group of living things that share similar characteristics and can breed with each other

2 **Match the descriptions and the pictures.**
1. ◯ It lives in water and eats small plants.
2. ◯ It lives in the South Pole and feeds on fish.
3. ◯ It can run fast and you can ride on its back.
4. ◯ It has colored wings and eats flower nectar.
5. ◯ It can change colors and look in two directions at once.
6. ◯ It can live at people's homes and is very friendly.

Be Strategic!
When you write, first make a plan. Decide what to write in each paragraph. Follow the rule: one idea, one paragraph.

3 **Write an essay about your favorite animal.**

Butterfly
b Chameleon

Dog
d Emperor Penguin

Goldfish
f Horse

4 **Write the questions. Interview your partner.**
1. what / favorite animal
   _____
2. what / look like
   _____
3. where / live
   _____
4. what / eat
   _____
5. it / endangered species
   _____
6. it / popular pet
   _____
7. why / your favorite
   _____

 Stop and Think! Why are animals important to our world?

Glossary
fur: the hair of an animal
habitat: the area where an animal lives
endangered species: an animal that might become extinct
wild: not controlled by people

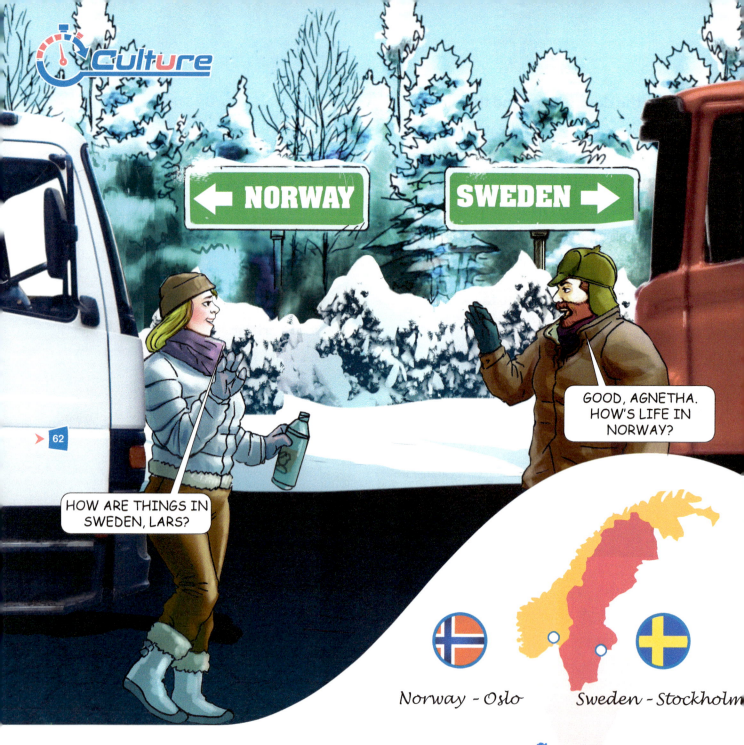

1 **Study the map. In your notebook, correct the false sentences.**

  1. The capital of Sweden is Norway.
  2. Both countries are in Europe.
  3. They are near the North Pole.
  4. Sweden and Norway share a **border**.

2 🎧¹⁶ **Listen and follow the comic. Then answer the questions.**

  1. How can you tell the people in the comic know each other?
  2. What's the weather like?
  3. What word does Lars use to describe the smell?
  4. What's Agnetha carrying in her truck?
  5. What does Sweden do with Norway's garbage?

3 **Choose the best summary.**

1. ☐ Lars and Agnetha drive trucks. They both come from the same country. Lars takes garbage to Norway because they need it to make energy.

2. ☐ Lars and Agnetha are meeting for the first time. Lars smells something bad in Agnetha's truck. He does not want this garbage to go to his country.

3. ☐ Lars and Agnetha are friends from different countries. Today Agnetha is carrying garbage in her truck. Sweden uses Norway's garbage to produce energy.

Stop and Think! How does recycling help the planet?

Glossary

border: the line that separates two countries

garbage: things you throw away

trash: another word for garbage

# Project

1 Read the post. Do you agree or disagree. Why?

Cassie Richards • 525 subscribers
2 minutes ago near Boston •

 Subscribe

My parents always put their garbage in the trash can and they always clean up, but who cares? If I'm chewing gum in the car, I just throw it out the window when I finish. If I have a can of soda on the train, I leave it on the seat. Someone else can clean it up. I'm very busy!

Like · Share   25

136 people like this.

2 Look at the poster. Answer the questions.
1. What does it show?
2. Are the rates exact?
3. What is the relationship between an item and the size of its picture?
4. Which item disappears faster?
5. Which is worse, a milk carton or an aluminum can?
6. Which items share a similar rate of decomposition?

3 Interview 10 classmates and complete the graph.

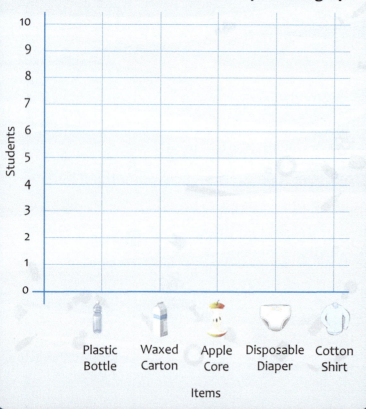

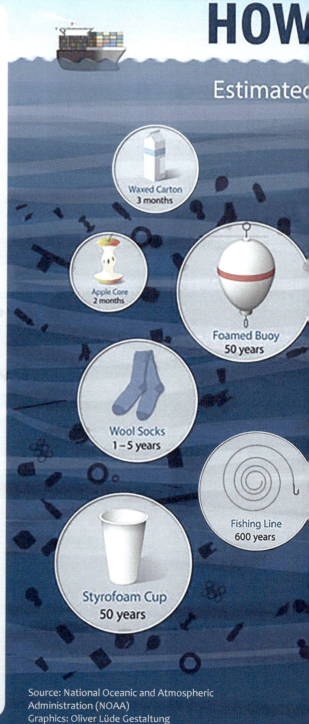

Source: National Oceanic and Atmospheric Administration (NOAA)
Graphics: Oliver Lüde Gestaltung

4 **Make a two-minute video to promote a green attitude. Follow these instructions.**

- Choose one of these topics:
  1. Recycling old clothes
  2. Returning old medicines to drugstores
  3. Recycling metal, plastic and glass
  4. Throwing garbage in proper containers
- Write a script. Everyone participates.
- Use images.
- Use a cell phone to make your video.
- Show it to the class.

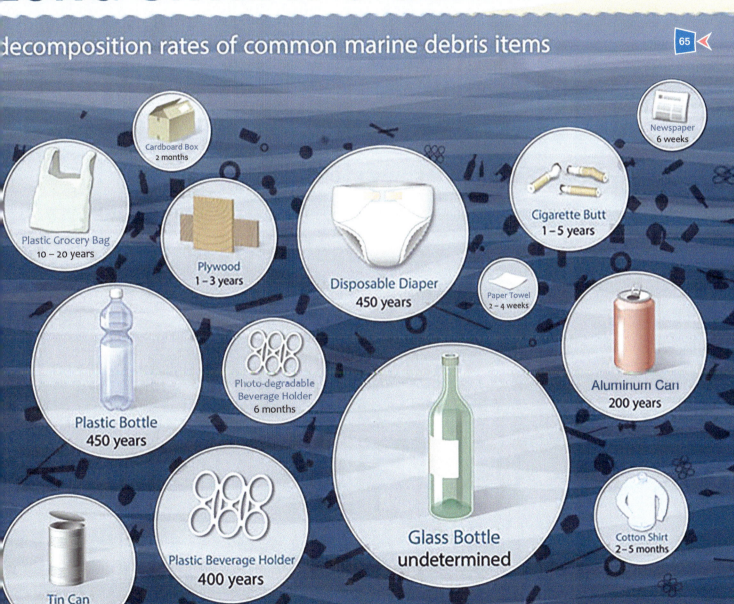

LONG UNTIL IT'S GONE?
decomposition rates of common marine debris items

Review

1 Complete the puzzle. What is the mystery food?

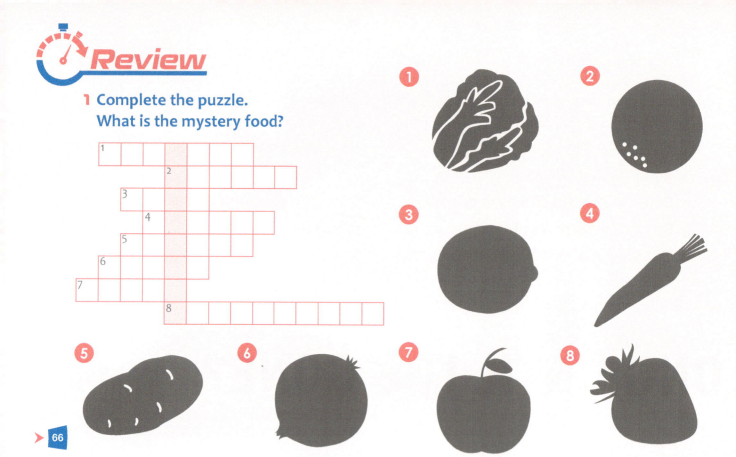

2 Complete the missing letters in the text.

Dear Diary,

My garden is full of (1) w___ds! I don't have any fruit or vegetables. I don't have a green (2) t_____b. Nothing goes right. The birds eat the (3) s___ds so no plants grow. The birds eat all the (4) e___ thw_____s too. I need them to help the plants grow.

But there is more. The (5) s_____ls eat my lettuces and the (6) c__t___p___l___s eat my strawberries. It's a disaster! I put (7) f___ t_____ z__r on the ground, but it doesn't help. Nothing grows. It also never rains, so I (8) w_____r the garden once a week, but all my plants are dying. The result? If you (9) d___ in the garden, you might find two or three tiny potatoes. You can (10) p___k one orange—one—from the tree! That's it! There's no fruit and no vegetables! It's a total disaster! I need help.

3 Read and complete the conversation.

any   little   few   lot   many   much   some

EMMA: Whew! Biking is hungry work! Colin, what drinks do we have?
COLIN: Umm… we don't have (1) _____ drinks.
EMMA: What?
COLIN: Well, I have a (2) _____ water in this bottle.
EMMA: How (3) _____ water is there?
COLIN: Just a drop. Look.
EMMA: Oh no! Well, OK. Let's eat the sandwiches.
COLIN: Sandwiches? I don't have (4) _____ sandwiches. I have (5) _____ bread. Oh, look. I have a (6) _____ carrots in my bag.
EMMA: Carrots? For lunch? How (7) _____ carrots do you have?
COLIN: 1, 2… 3. They're very good for you.
EMMA: Great work, Colin. Water, bread and three carrots. What a lunch!
COLIN: Sorry, Emma. My bag's really heavy.
EMMA: Don't worry, Colin. Pass me some bread.
COLIN: Here you go.

4 Correct the mistakes.

1. Get a few lettuce for the salad.
   _____
2. How many spaghetti do you want?
   _____
3. There's only a few rice. Can you go to the store, please?
   _____
4. How many butter do you put on your toast?
   _____
5. We don't have some cherries.
   _____
6. How much apples do you have for the pie?
   _____

5 Complete these sentences about you.

1. I have a lot of _____ at home.
2. There aren't any _____ in my hometown.
3. I usually eat a little _____ every day.
4. We have some _____ at my school.
5. I usually have a few _____ in my bag.
6. There isn't any _____ in the fridge at home.

Just for Fun

1 Find 11 countable and uncountable nouns. Then classify them.

```
I Q T S U G A R S V
I K O M I L K C A O
U B M A C D P A P N
O R A N G E S R O I
J F T F L O U R T O
T K O G F I P O A N
B R E A D L H T T S
K F S X C U Q S O V
C O F F E E I R E W
C H E R R I E S S U
```

Countable	Uncountable

2 Look and write the names of the animals.

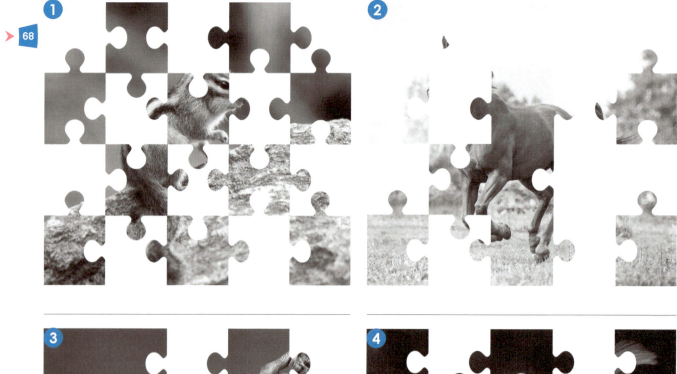

1 🎧17 **Listen and label the pictures.**

camping   dancing   doing cannonballs   drawing   hanging out with friends
making models   playing board games   popping a wheelie   rollerblading

2 Copy the pastimes onto the chart in your notebook. Then complete it.

	camping	dancing...
individual		
in groups		
done outdoors		
done indoors		
very active		
dangerous		

3 Think Fast! Add two more pastimes to the chart.

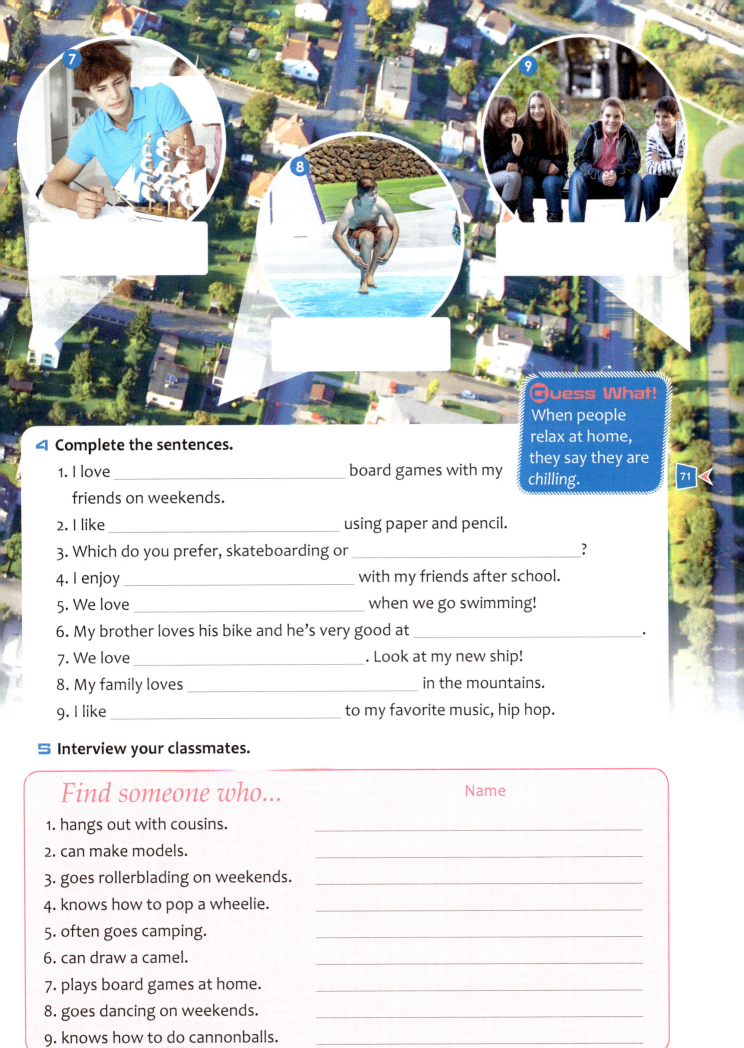

4 Complete the sentences.

1. I love _____ board games with my friends on weekends.
2. I like _____ using paper and pencil.
3. Which do you prefer, skateboarding or _____?
4. I enjoy _____ with my friends after school.
5. We love _____ when we go swimming!
6. My brother loves his bike and he's very good at _____.
7. We love _____. Look at my new ship!
8. My family loves _____ in the mountains.
9. I like _____ to my favorite music, hip hop.

Guess What! When people relax at home, they say they are *chilling*.

5 Interview your classmates.

Find someone who...   Name

1. hangs out with cousins.
2. can make models.
3. goes rollerblading on weekends.
4. knows how to pop a wheelie.
5. often goes camping.
6. can draw a camel.
7. plays board games at home.
8. goes dancing on weekends.
9. knows how to do cannonballs.

Grammar

1 🎧¹⁸ **Listen and complete the sentences.**

My grandmother **was** three in this picture. She **wasn't** sad at her (1) _____ party. She **was** very happy. Here, my grandma and her friends **were** in (2) _____ grade. They **weren't** in high school yet. In this picture, my grandfather **wasn't** angry. He **was** just (3) _____. This **was** my grandfather's typewriter. It **wasn't** (4) _____ like a computer. Look at this! I **was** two in this picture. We **were** at my grandmother's (5) _____ in LA.

2 **Read the sentences above and number the pictures.**

Verb *be: was, were*
I was(n't). She was(n't).
They were(n't).

3 **Look at the pictures and circle the correct options.**
   1. My grandfather **was / were** a serious guy at school.
   2. I **was / were** always happy with my grandmother.
   3. She **wasn't / weren't** next to her dad in that picture.
   4. My grandma's friends **wasn't / weren't** very short in 8ᵗʰ grade.

4 **Look at the photo. Decide if the sentences are T (True) or F (False).**
   1. There weren't any computers.   T   F
   2. There was a TV in the classroom.   T   F
   3. There were cell phones.   T   F
   4. There wasn't a map.   T   F

5 **Think Fast!** What was there in your classroom in primary school?

6 **Use *was* or *were* to complete the questions. Then answer the questions in your notebook.**
   1. Where _____ you at 2 p.m. yesterday?
   2. Who _____ your best friend in primary school?
   3. _____ you late for school today?
   4. _____ there any homework yesterday?

Reading & Speaking

1 Read the e-mail and number the pictures.

Mail

Hi!

What a weekend! We rode the **roller coasters at an amusement park**. It was a lot of fun!

Here are some pictures. In the first one, my friends Pedro and Melanie are **in the front**. Pedro is **on the left**. He's wearing a yellow T-shirt. Melanie is on the right. She has long blonde hair.

In the second photo, I look scared! My friend Sean is sitting **next to me**. He has on a white T-shirt and a yellow vest. You can also see Arturo. He's **behind Pedro**. He's in a red T-shirt.

The last photo is the best one! Sean and I are in the front. Melanie and Pedro are **in the middle**. And my cousin Wendy is **in the back**. She's in a gray T-shirt and she has her hands up in the air. She looks nervous!

Speak soon!

Tania

2 Read the e-mail again and label the people.

74

Be Strategic!
When you describe a photo, first study it for a moment. Then plan a coherent way for your listener to understand what is in the picture. Use adjectives and expressions of place.

Glossary
roller coaster:
amusement park:

3 Look at the highlighted phrases in the e-mail and complete the expressions below.

1. at _____
2. in the _____
3. on the _____
4. next to _____
5. behind _____
6. in the _____
7. in the _____

4 Choose a photo and describe it to your partner. Your partner points at the correct picture.

Stop and Think! Are friends important to make you happy?

75

Culture

1 Read the introduction of the article and complete the mind map.

- Arabian Peninsula
- largest country
- capital
- language
- produces
- weekends are on
- average temperature
- desert people called

2 Read the article on page 77 and mark (✓) the topics mentioned.

1. ☐ hobbies
2. ☐ animals
3. ☐ language
4. ☐ family
5. ☐ hospitality
6. ☐ schools

Life in the Desert

The Arabian Peninsula consists of seven countries, Kuwait, Bahrain, Qatar, United Arab Emirates, Saudi Arabia, Oman, Yemen and parts of Jordan and Iraq. The biggest country in the Arabian peninsula is Saudi Arabia. Its capital city is Riyadh. It is one of the world's richest countries because it produces lots of oil. Much of the country is desert and it gets very hot. The average temperature in summer is over 40°C! In Saudi Arabia, weekends are Friday and Saturday. People speak Arabic. Many of its cities are very modern, but other people still live a simpler life in the desert: these people are nomads called the Bedouin, "the desert **dwellers**."

Desert People

In the deserts of Arabia, there are people who live in **tents** and travel from place to place. These are the Bedouins, a group of people who honor tradition, respect and hard work.

The Bedouin family is where children learn the values of the community. The father is the living example for children. They learn to listen to elders and to follow the strict rules of their **clan**.

Animals are an important part of their lives and families. Camels provide transportation, milk, food and clothing. Bedouins learn to treat them with respect and even consider them part of the family. Camels have their own personalities that can even resemble their owners'! For Bedouins, camels are "the ship of the desert" and a "gift from God."

Hospitality in a Bedouin clan is crucial. The hard conditions of life in the desert make strong family ties and also motivate a strong sense of hospitality towards other desert travelers. It is always a big event to see a stranger in the quiet and lonely desert landscape. According to their beliefs, a guest should always be treated with respect and kindness.

The Bedouin people are warm and kind with a strong sense of community, honor and respect towards others. They are an example of traditions that extend over time.

3 Read again and answer the questions in your notebook.

1. Do Bedouin people have a permanent home?
2. What is the importance of the Bedouin family?
3. What four things do camels provide?
4. Why are camels considered a "ship" and a "gift"?
5. How do Bedouins feel about other people in the desert?

 Stop and Think! How does taking care of others make you happy?

Glossary

dweller: a person who lives in a particular place

tent: a structure made of cloth and poles where people can live

clan: a large group of families related to each other

# Project

Happiness is not something **ready** made. It comes from your **own actions**.
—Dalai Lama

1 Read the quotes. Circle the one you like best. What's the most popular one in the class?

 2 Think Fast! List five things that make you happy.

3 Read the survey report on the next page and circle T (True) or F (False).

1. The size of the sample was 15 students.   T   F
2. Most students feel happy with their families.   T   F
3. Teachers are the second preferred choice.   T   F
4. Only some students like having their own bedroom.   T   F
5. Students think money makes them happy.   T   F
6. Students prefer social media over the radio.   T   F

4 In your notebook, change the highlighted fractions in the survey to percentages.

5 Design a survey report on what makes teenagers happy. Follow these instructions.
- Use the questions and options from the survey report on page 79.
- Interview students in your school or in your class.
- Prepare pie charts to present the information.
- Write a survey report.

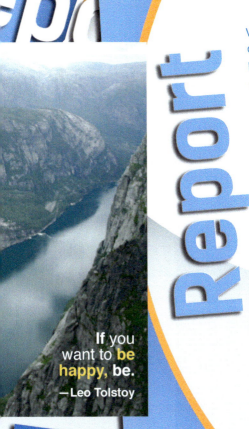

> If you want to **be happy**, be.
> —Leo Tolstoy

Report

We want to know what makes teenagers happy. To find out, we have four questions in the following categories: relationships, belongings, money & popularity and technology. Our sample consists of 24 students, ages 13 to 15.

In terms of relationships, **one-half** of the students say their families are important to their happiness. **One-fourth** of the sample considers best friends as factors of happiness.

In the category of belongings, **two-thirds** of the students say having their own bedroom makes them feel good and comfortable. This result is larger than for any of the other options: having a bike, a pet or a new video game.

Our third question is about social perception. **Three-quarters** of the sample state that grades have a positive influence on their feelings. For them, getting good grades and making their families and themselves proud are sources of happiness. Others consider popularity at school important, and only a small number of students consider money as the way to feel happy.

Finally, there is the aspect of technology in students' lives. For **one-third** of the sample, social media is very important and makes them feel closer to their family and friends. Students are also interested in the latest gadgets. It is interesting to see that radio and television are not the top choices among students' preferences, but they are still present.

Conclusion
From our questionnaire, we can see that teenagers in our school feel that happiness involves spending time with their families, having their own personal space, achieving at school and staying in touch with loved ones through social media.

Report

1. Who are the most important people in your life?
   - family
   - best friends
   - classmates
   - teachers

2. Which of these things makes you happier?
   - own bedroom
   - own bike
   - a pet
   - a new video game

3. Which of these things is most important for you?
   - money
   - popularity
   - beauty
   - good grades

4. Which of the following is your favorite?
   - social media
   - phones/tablets
   - radio
   - television

Review

1 Follow and write the activities.

2 Cross out the options that don't belong.

1. I usually **play board games** / **make models** on my own.
2. I feel hungry after **dancing** / **drawing** because it's a lot of exercise.
3. I usually **do cannonballs** / **play board games** in the living room.
4. Nick always does crazy things like **doing cannonballs** / **hanging out**.
5. I love **camping** / **hanging out** with my friends in the café.
6. My hobby is **making models** / **rollerblading** because I love being outdoors.
7. It's a lot of fun **doing cannonballs** / **popping a wheelie** at the swimming pool.
8. My blog is about people on wheels, like **dancing** / **rollerblading**.

3 Circle the correct options.

1. I **was** / **were** late for class this morning.
2. My brothers **was** / **were** at the soccer match last weekend.
3. We **wasn't** / **weren't** at school last week.
4. **Was** / **Were** you at the mall last Saturday?
5. How many people **was** / **were** in your class last year?
6. My mom **wasn't** / **weren't** happy with my grades last year.
7. I **wasn't** / **weren't** in your class last year.
8. There **wasn't** / **weren't** any children at the party last night.

4 Complete the conversation with *was* or *were* in the correct form.

How ¹_____ the swimming pool yesterday?

Terrible! There ²_____ hundreds of people there because it ³_____ a very hot day.

Oh no! I'm happy I ⁴_____ there. ⁵_____ you with Mel and Viv?

No, they ⁶_____ at the pool. They ⁷_____ in an exam.

Too bad for them! ⁸_____ Isabel with you?

Yes, she ⁹_____. She ¹⁰_____ red at the end of the day.

Red? Why?

There ¹¹_____ any sunscreen and we ¹²_____ in the sun all day.

That's crazy!

I know. At the end, her face ¹³_____ red but her eyes ¹⁴_____ white—because of her sunglasses!

5 Complete the description with the words below.

back   left   middle   right   top

This is a picture of me and my friends. It's a volleyball game! At the (1) _____ there's the ball. I'm on the (2) _____ in the blue shirt. My sister is in the (3) _____ with her friend Janet. On the (4) _____ of the picture is Ian. He always falls down on the sand! He's a terrible volleyball player! My best friend Harry is in the (5) _____ in the pink and white shirt. He's crazy! What's your favorite picture of your friends?

6 Complete these sentences so they are true for you.

1. My favorite board game is _____.
2. I am very good at drawing _____.
3. I want to go camping in _____.
4. My favorite music for dancing is _____.
5. I usually hang out with my friends _____.

Just for Fun

1 What's the pastime?

1. _____

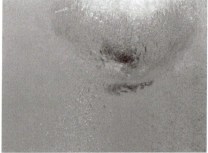
2. _____

3. _____

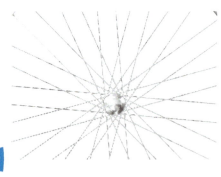
4. _____

5. _____

6. _____

7. _____

8. _____

9. _____

2 Unscramble the words.

1. (s d e e r t) _____
2. (c a i r a b) _____
3. (m e c a l) _____
4. (d e b o n u i) _____
5. (d a i s u b a i a r a) _____
6. (d f i a y r) _____

3 Complete the sentences with the unscrambled words from Activity 2.

1. The nomads in the Arabian Peninsula are called _____.
2. The largest country in the Arabian Peninsula is _____.
3. People in the Arabian Peninsula speak _____.
4. Many people live in the _____.
5. The _____ is the "ship of the desert."
6. Weekends are on _____ and Saturday there.

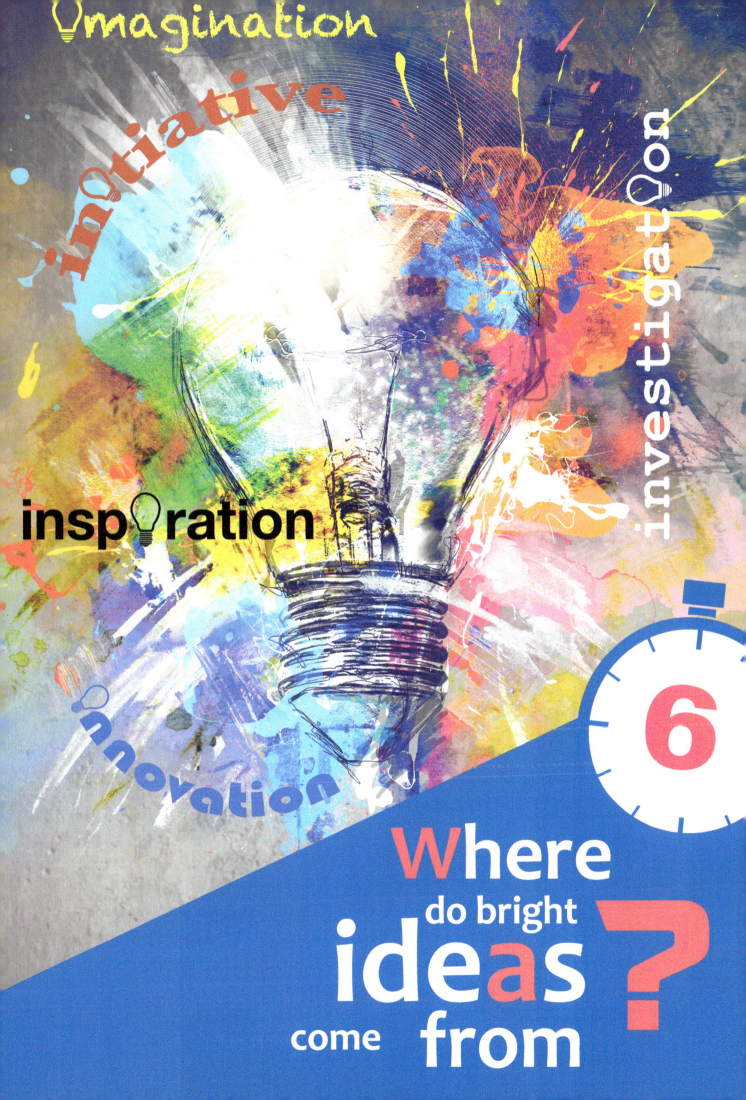

Vocabulary

1 Decode the missing verbs. (43 = S, 15 = E, etc.)

This is Kelly Reese and her invention—a rug for elderly sick people. The rug activates an alarm when an elderly, sick person gets up from bed at night. Relatives

Kelly was **worried about** her grandma. How could she help?

1 __ __ __ a question
   11 43 25

For several months, she was **busy with** her research. So many ideas!

2 __ __ research
   14 34

She was **interested in** a special rug with a sensor to detect her grandma's feet. Was it possible

3 __ __ __ __ __ a hypothesis
   52 42 24 44 15

2 Match the steps of the scientific method above to their explanation.
a. ☐ To express your explanation or solution to a problem in a clear sentence.
b. ☐ To conduct a very careful plan to test that your idea is valid.
c. ☐ To investigate to find out more about the situation or problem.
d. ☐ To state a question about a problem.
e. ☐ To study the information collected in an experiment.
f. ☐ To make a summary of the results and relate them to your hypothesis.

3 Identify and number the events according to the scientific method.
☐ Tomatoes on our family farm did not grow well this season.
☐ We can say that tomato plants with the most water grew the biggest. So, the hypothesis is true.
☐ We plant tomatoes in areas with the same amount of light each day. Each plant receives different amounts of water. We record the size of the tomatoes when they start to grow.
☐ We notice that the tomato plants receiving a cup of water every day grew to 1.27 cm in diameter. Tomatoes receiving two cups of water grew to 1.90 cm in diameter.
☐ We think the tomatoes did not grow well because there wasn't much rain.
☐ Why did our tomatoes not grow well this season?

Stop and Think! When do you feel inspired to solve a problem?

f the elderly person receive the
arm and can go and check that
e person is safe. Kelly Reese got
spiration from her grandmother
ho suffers from dementia.

SCIENTIFIC METHOD

She was **nervous about** her prototype. The rug and the sensors were ready.

4 ___ ___ an experiment
   14 34

Kelly is **good at** numbers. The results of the experiment were good!

5 ___ ___ ___ ___ ___ ___ ___ data
   11 33 11 31 54 55 15

She was **excited about** the results. The electronic rug worked. Grandma was safe!

6 ___ ___ ___ ___ conclusions
   14 42 11 52

4 Complete the mind map with the highlighted expressions in Activity 1.

Adjectives and prepositions
- good
- about
- with

5 Answer the questions.

1. What were you worried about last week? _____
2. What are you busy with in the afternoons? _____
3. What hobby or sport are you interested in? _____
4. What are you sometimes nervous about? _____
5. What subject were you good at last year? _____
6. What movie are you excited about? _____

85

Grammar

1 🎧 19 **Listen and complete the sentences.**

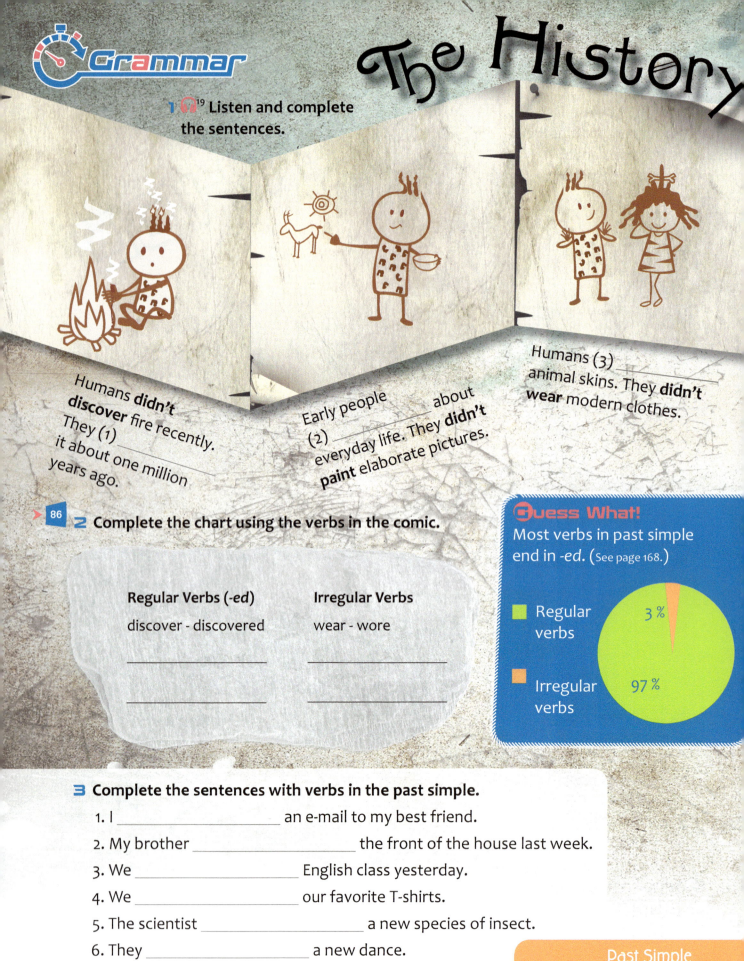

Humans **didn't discover** fire recently. They (1) _____ it about one million years ago.

Early people (2) _____ about everyday life. They **didn't paint** elaborate pictures.

Humans (3) _____ animal skins. They **didn't wear** modern clothes.

2 Complete the chart using the verbs in the comic.

Regular Verbs (-ed)	Irregular Verbs
discover - discovered	wear - wore
_____	_____
_____	_____

Guess What!
Most verbs in past simple end in -ed. (See page 168.)

- Regular verbs — 97 %
- Irregular verbs — 3 %

3 Complete the sentences with verbs in the past simple.

1. I _____ an e-mail to my best friend.
2. My brother _____ the front of the house last week.
3. We _____ English class yesterday.
4. We _____ our favorite T-shirts.
5. The scientist _____ a new species of insect.
6. They _____ a new dance.

4 In your notebook, write the sentences above in negative form.

Past Simple - Auxiliary

Use **didn't** (did not) for negative sentences.
Use **did** for questions.

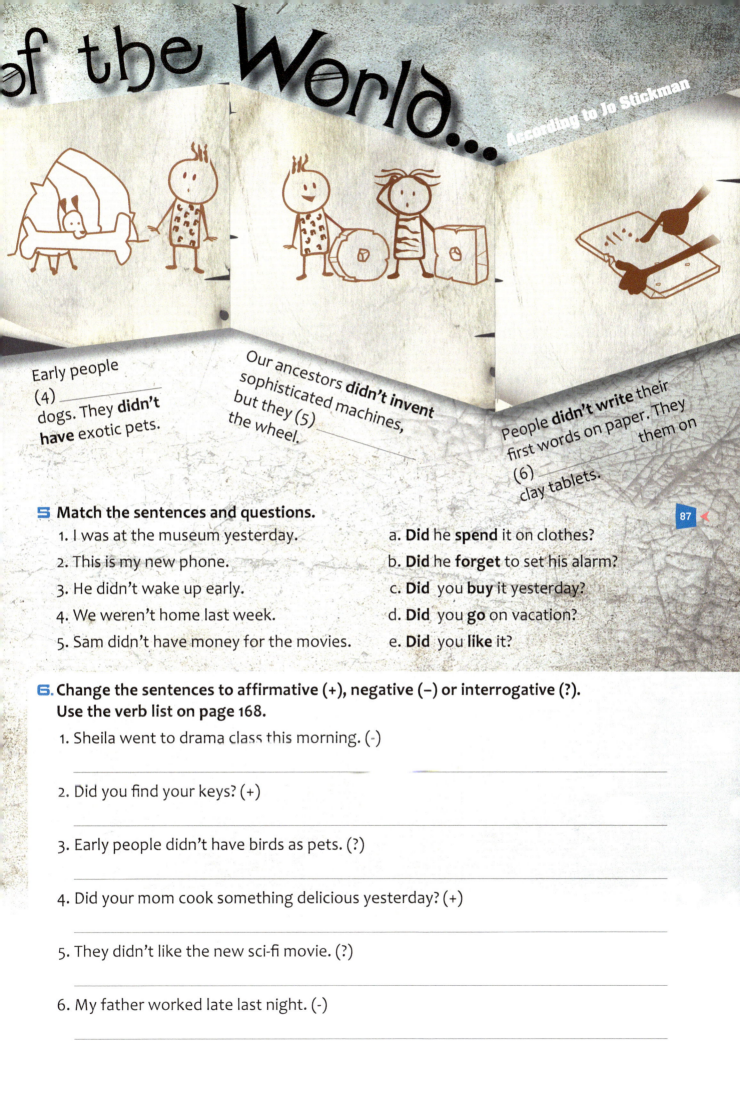

Early people (4) _____ dogs. They **didn't have** exotic pets.

Our ancestors **didn't invent** sophisticated machines, but they (5) _____ the wheel.

People **didn't write** their first words on paper. They (6) _____ them on clay tablets.

5 Match the sentences and questions.
1. I was at the museum yesterday.
2. This is my new phone.
3. He didn't wake up early.
4. We weren't home last week.
5. Sam didn't have money for the movies.

a. **Did** he **spend** it on clothes?
b. **Did** he **forget** to set his alarm?
c. **Did** you **buy** it yesterday?
d. **Did** you **go** on vacation?
e. **Did** you **like** it?

6. Change the sentences to affirmative (+), negative (−) or interrogative (?). Use the verb list on page 168.

1. Sheila went to drama class this morning. (−)

2. Did you find your keys? (+)

3. Early people didn't have birds as pets. (?)

4. Did your mom cook something delicious yesterday? (+)

5. They didn't like the new sci-fi movie. (?)

6. My father worked late last night. (−)

Listening and Writing

> **Be Strategic!**
> Before you listen to a podcast or video, make a note of words and names that might appear on the recording. This helps you anticipate what is on the recording.

1 Complete the mind map with five words related to Steve Jobs.

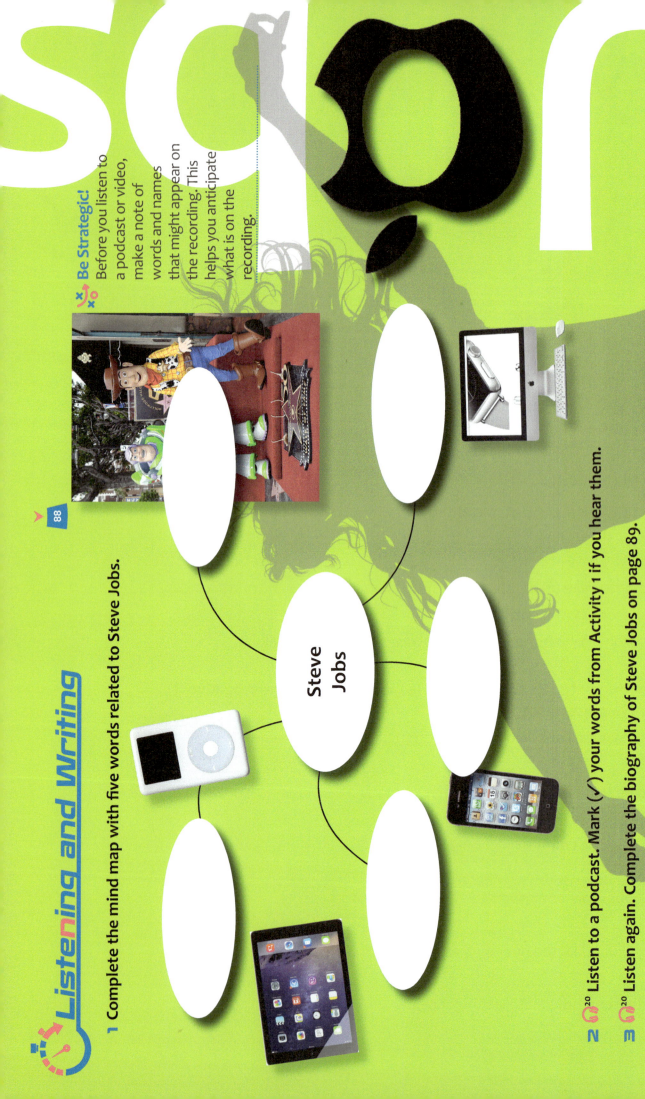

2 🎧²⁰ Listen to a podcast. Mark (✓) your words from Activity 1 if you hear them.

3 🎧²⁰ Listen again. Complete the biography of Steve Jobs on page 89.

88

Creativity at Its Finest: **Steve Jobs**

Steve Jobs was born in San Francisco on February 24th (1) _____ . In (2) _____ Steve Jobs had a summer job at Hewlett Packard. He met Steve Wozniak there. In (3) _____ , Steve Wozniak invented his first computer.

Then in (4) _____ , he and Jobs started their own company, Apple. He worked there until (5) _____ . Jobs joined the movie studio Pixar in (6) _____ . Apple Jobs returned to Apple in (7) _____ . Apple produced the iPod in (8) _____ . In (9) _____ , Jobs discovered he had cancer, but he continued working. Apple invented the iPhone and it first appeared in (10) _____ . Then in (11) _____ they invented the iPad, Apple's first tablet. Tragically, Steve Jobs died on October 5th (12) _____ . He was one of the greatest minds of this century.

◀ **4 Write a biography.** Use the text in Activity 3 as a guide. Follow the instructions below.

- Choose a famous person. Do not choose a person who is alive today.
- Research the events of his / her life.
- Write the biography. Write the events in order from birth to death.
- Explain why the person is famous.
- Include any other interesting information.

Stop and Think! What type of personality is needed to produce good ideas?

Culture

1 Read and label the map using the highlighted names in the text.

Chile

Chile extends along most of the western coast of South America. It has a population of 15 million people. The main language is Spanish.

Chile extends over a long distance north to south, so it has many different climates. In the north, there is the **Atacama Desert**, the driest place on Earth. Chile also has mountains. **The Andes** form the border between Chile and its neighbors Peru, Bolivia and Argentina.

The center of the country has a mild climate and most people live there, in and around the capital **Santiago**.

The south is cold and wet. Chile ends at **Cape Horn**, the most southern point in South America. Cape Horn is a place that is famous for its rough seas and dangerous passage by sea.

2 🎧²¹ Look at the photos. Then listen and answer the questions.
1. What part of Chile is this?
2. Are they telescopes or radars?
3. What is the purpose of this project?

3 🎧²¹ Listen again and correct the false information in each sentence.
1. The desert is 10 square kilometers and nobody lives here.
2. The Atacama Desert is the home of Alma, an international project to study the fauna.
3. It's very dry, so there aren't many birds in the sky.
4. We have ten tiny and very powerful telescopes here.
5. We need the money of experts from all around the world.
6. Alma's work in Chile is an example of national collaboration.

4 Think Fast! Try to solve the puzzle on your own.

This is a cow. It has its body, horns, legs and tail. Move two matches so that the cow is looking to the right.

5 Do the puzzle above in small groups. Check your answer on page 96. Then answer the questions.

1. Was it easier to find a solution on your own or in groups?
2. What advantages are there in working in groups?
3. What do you need to work effectively in groups?

Project

1 Read the ad and complete the information.

Mars

Mars is the closest planet to earth and it's possible to see it in the night sky with the naked eye. People knew of its existence in ancient times. The planet is named Mars after the Roman God of War. It has two moons: Phobos and Deimos.

The Red Planet

A day on Mars is almost the same as on earth, 24 hours and 37 minutes. Its year is much longer: 687 Earth days. Mars is about 235 million kilometers from Earth. It takes nine months to travel there.

Mission to Mars

We want to start a colony on the planet Mars. The journey is nine months on a spacecraft with three other people. After you arrive on Mars, you live there for a year. Don't miss the opportunity! Apply for the program now!

MARS
Named after _____
Number of moons _____
Length of day _____
Length of year _____
Distance from Earth _____
Time needed to arrive there _____

2 🎧²² Listen and label the objects on the next page.

3 Work in groups. Follow the instructions.
- Mark (✓) the six most important items to take on your trip to Mars.
- Think of an advantage and a disadvantage of taking each object.
- Prepare a poster with your six choices. Share it with the class.

4 🎧²³ Listen to an expert choose six items. Did you choose the same objects?

Review

1 Complete the flowchart for the scientific method.

conclusions   data   experiment   hypothesis   question   research

1. ask a
2. do
3. write a
4. do an
5. analyze
6. draw

2 Choose the correct options to complete the sentences.

1. I was busy *about / with* homework and couldn't go to the movies.
2. My brother was excited *from / about* his trip to New York.
3. What are you good *at / in*?
4. Paul and Gino are interested *in / on* a new video game.
5. Were you nervous *of / about* the final math exam?
6. My dad was worried *about / on* our sick dog.

3 Rewrite the sentences in the past simple.

1. We cook an omelet for lunch.
   _____

2. Does Fiona watch TV with you?
   _____

3. Adam doesn't like the movie.
   _____

4. Denise and Joan don't play volleyball.
   _____

5. Do you walk to school?
   _____

6. Chris looks tired.
   _____

4 Complete the crossword with the past simple of these irregular verbs.

Down ↓
2. see
3. begin
5. think
7. have
8. drive
9. make
12. get

Across →
1. lose
4. write
6. wear
7. hear
9. meet
10. put
11. do
13. choose
14. speak

5 Complete the interview with the correct forms of the verbs in parentheses.

Q: What (1) _____ (be) the California Gold Rush?
A: It was a time when thousands of people (2) _____ (go) to California to look for gold.
Q: When (3) _____ the Gold Rush _____ (begin)?
A: In 1848, James W. Marshall (4) _____ (discover) gold at Sutter's Mill in California. Soon thousands of people (5) _____ (arrive) in California—they all (6) _____ (want) gold!

Q: When (7) _____ it _____ (end)?
A: The Gold Rush (8) _____ (end) seven years later, in 1855. Most people (9) _____ (not / find) any gold and they (10) _____ (not / become) rich. Many people actually (11) _____ (lose) money. It was just a crazy time when hundreds of people (12) _____ (get) gold fever all at the same time!

6 Use the words below and add more to write sentences in the past that are true for you.

1. I / meet / my best friend
   _____

2. I / start / school
   _____

3. this morning / I / eat / for breakfast
   _____

4. yesterday I / watch / on TV
   _____

5. last week / I / didn't
   _____

6. last weekend / I / go
   _____

Just for Fun

1 Complete the clues. Then find the words in the puzzle.

1. Ask a _____
2. Do _____
3. Write a _____
4. Do an _____
5. _____ data
6. Draw _____

```
C A F R S X H Q M H K U
C O Z G P D U W Y Y E Q
S D N I C E T P E Z B E
P N D C S O O H Y Y J X
K B W T L T M L W U S P
D M I H H U A K R G D E
N O L E W N S Y Q T C R
N S S Z A V P I J V T I
Y I H V X G G J O A X M
S R E S E A R C H N Q E
Q J R H Z R U W N O S N
D F V X O W F Q T E Y T
```

2 Unscramble the verbs in present simple. Then write them in past simple form.

Present Simple   **Past Simple**

1. (n i b g e) _____   __ __ __ __ __
                              1   8

2. (r e v d i s o c) _____   __ __ __ __ __ __ __ __
                                    7   3   5

3. (e r a h) _____   __ __ __ __ __
                              2

4. (r e w i t) _____   __ __ __ __ __
                               6   4

3 Complete the word using the letters from Activity 2.

Plastic bags normally take 10 – 20 years to decompose. But when Daniel Burd put a plastic bag in a solution of dirt, yeast and water for three months, he made a surprising discovery—the bag decomposed! What's the secret?

__ __ __ __ __ __ __ __ !
1 2 3 4 5 6 7 8

4 Answer the riddle.

What did Mars say to Saturn?

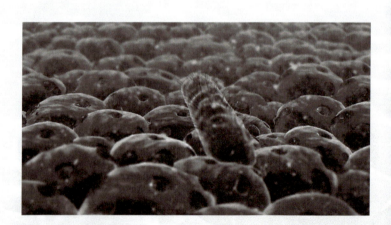

Answer to puzzle on page 91

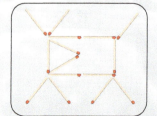

NEWS

Weather Forecast

It'll be snowy in Vancouver today. There will be a meter of snow in some parts of the city. Temperatures around -10.

Moving south, temperatures will be warmer in New York, but it'll be rainy. The rain will start in the early morning and carry on all day. Philadelphia will be dry but foggy. Driving in fog can be very dangerous in this area, especially early in the morning.

Staying in the US, LA will be warm but cloudy. Clouds may disappear by lunchtime and it will be sunny in the afternoon. So enjoy the sun! In Texas, there are strong winds and the windy weather will be especially bad in Dallas.

Finally, moving south into Mexico, the storm season arrived. Mexico City will have very stormy weather, especially in the evening, so make sure you have an umbrella if you're in the capital in the afternoon.

98

Vocabulary

1 Complete the chart using words in the weather forecast.

Symbol	Noun	Adjective
1. ❄	snow	
2. 💧	rain	
3. ☀		foggy
4. ☁	cloud	
5. ☀		sunny
6. 💨	wind	
7. ⚡		stormy

2 Complete the sentences using the adjectives in Activity 1.

1. He can't see because it's ___.

2. He's scared because it's ___.

Guess What!
The four seasons are spring, summer, fall (autumn) and winter.

4 🎧²⁴ **Listen again and circle the mistake in each sentence. Rewrite the sentences.**

1. It's spring in Australia and temperatures are very different across the continent.

   _____

2. It'll be 13° C and sunny all day in Rome.

   _____

3. The storms will end in the early morning in Madrid.

   _____

4. It's a foggy, warm day in London.

   _____

5. Berlin will be warm, 22° C but rainy.

   _____

6. It's cloudy all over Moscow.

   _____

5 Think Fast! What's the best time of year to visit your country?

3 min

3. He can't walk the dog because it's

4. He's not enjoying the beach because it's

5. He lost his cap because it's

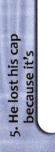

6. His barbecue isn't a success because it's

7. His ice cream is melting because it's

3 🎧²⁴ **Listen to the world weather forecast. Mark (✓) the weather you hear.**

	☀️	❄️	⛈️	💧	☁️	☀️
Rome						
Madrid						
London						
Berlin						
Paris						
Moscow						

99

Grammar

1 Read the forecast and trace the trajectory of the hurricane on the map.

Q & A: All About Hurricane Julia

Q: Where is Hurricane Julia now?

A: At the moment it is just north of Puerto Rico. The storm **will move** west, across the Turks and Caicos Islands. But it **won't stay** there, it **will travel** north of the Bahamas.

Q: **Will** it **be** dangerous for people in the Bahamas?

A: No, because it **won't hit** the islands. At least not directly, but it **will rain** a lot.

Q: Where **will** it **head** next?

A: Julia **will travel** west and **hit** the east coast of the US

Q: **Will** it **affect** Miami?

A: Yes, **it will**. **It'll move** through Miami and straight into the Gulf of Mexico.

Q: And then where **will** Julia **go**?

A: We think Julia **will hit** Louisiana and **will move** north of New Orleans. It **won't affect** the nearby states except for the heavy rain.

Guess What!
Hurricanes and storms always have short names. There is an official list of male and female names for them.

Future Simple

It **will rain** hard.

They **won't go** out.

Will they **get** wet?

Note: Use future simple to predict events.

2 Complete the sentences using *will* or *won't*.

1. Hurricane Julia _____ pass across the Turks and Caicos Islands.
2. The hurricane _____ stay at the Bahamas.
3. In the Bahamas, the weather _____ be rainy.
4. Hurricane Julia _____ hit Miami.
5. It _____ move to Louisiana.
6. Experts expect Julia _____ be a problem for neighboring states.

3 Read and complete the sentences with the future simple.

1. Don't eat too much cake. You _____ sick.
2. It's rainy and windy today. _____ it _____ cold tomorrow?
3. My brother practices swimming every day. _____ he _____ the competition?
4. You broke your sister's favorite cup! She _____ very angry.
5. It's very hot outside today. We _____ to the supermarket.
6. Stop popping wheelies! You _____ an accident.

4 Read the post and complete the mind map.

Sam Horton: How **are** you **going to prepare** for Hurricane Julia? **Are** you **going to leave** town? What are your plans?
Like · Comment · Share · August 9 at 8:40 am
👍 25 people like this.

PJ: No, I'm not. **I'm going to stay,** but **I'm going to board up** my windows. A hurricane can break the glass and that's dangerous. It's a race against time but **I'm not going to worry** about it. We often have hurricanes over here!
August 9 at 9:01 am · Like · 👍 2

Silvia: Yes, I am. We**'re going to go** to our sister's house in Texas. The hurricane **isn't going to pass** over their house, so it's a safe place for me and my brothers.
August 9 at 9:17 am · Like · 👍 1

Future with *going to*

He**'s going to board up** his windows.
(be) (going to) (verb)

Mind map:
- PJ → _____
- Silvia → _____ in Texas.
- me → _____

5 Read the notes and write plans using *going to*.

1 Simone
Call Grandma (birthday on Friday!)
_____

2 Donnie and me
Guitar for music lesson after school
_____

3 Dad
Flight NY to Chicago 3pm Saturday
_____

4 Bobby and Helen
American Idol – TV tonight 7pm!!
_____

6 Write the sentences in Activity 5 in negative and interrogative forms in your notebook.

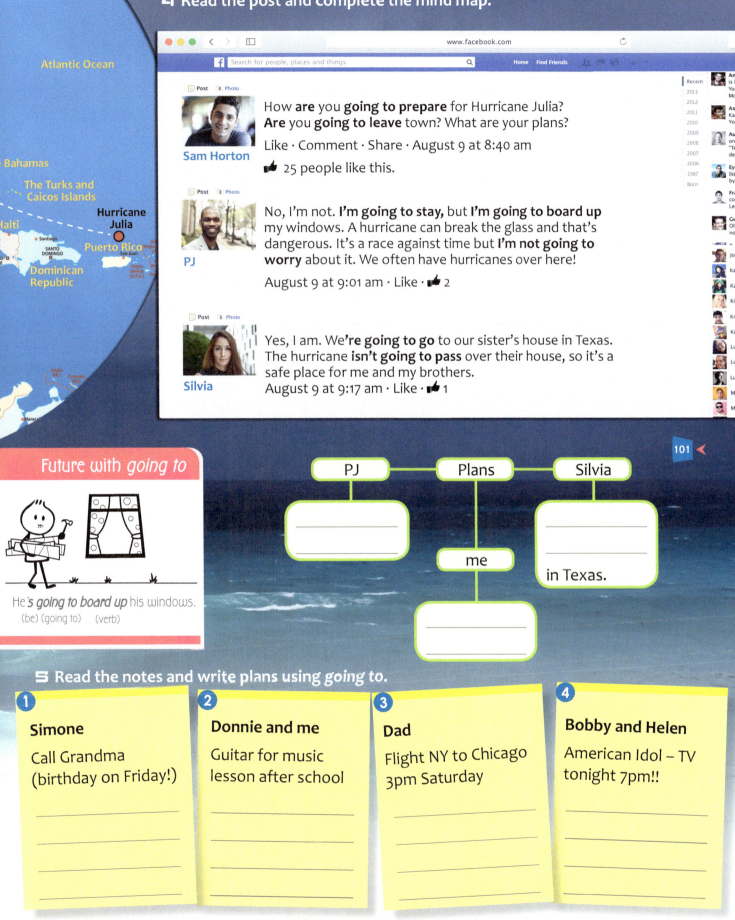

Reading & Speaking

1 Look at the title and the pictures. Answer the questions.

1. Do you think this will be a short story or a newspaper article?
2. What will you read about?
3. What weather words will appear in the article?

Be Strategic!
Before you read a text, look carefully at the title and the pictures. What information do they give you? Use them to predict the content.

DAILY NEWS

Gouldburn covered in spiderwebs.

Fields of spider webs

It's Raining Spiders!

For Bruce Cooke of Goulburn Australia, it all started with a strange feeling in his ear early in the morning.

"Something touched my ear and I thought, oh no, it's going to rain."

Unfortunately for Mr. Cooke, when he looked up at the sky, he saw a vision from his worst **nightmares**.

"It was raining spiders," he says with a **shudder** as if the weather suddenly turned cold.

Web curtains

"Millions of tiny spiders were falling from the sky."

Bruce, 43, is an arachnophobe. He doesn't like spiders at all. He ran indoors and closed all the doors and windows. The next morning, the whole town was white. It looked like snow, but actually spiderwebs covered the streets and homes.

It's like something out of a horror movie, but this rain of spiders is a real scientific fact. How did it happen?

Some spiders use their webs to make little parachutes. They use these parachutes to travel in the wind. It is a very common behavior, but people do not usually notice it, because there are only one or two spiders in the sky.

Sometimes millions of spiders travel simultaneously, and on a very windy day, all the animals arrive at the same place at the same time. That is what happened in Goulburn in May.

Thankfully, scientists say that this is a very rare event, so it is safe for Bruce Cooke to leave his house again.

2 Read the article and underline evidence to prove these facts.
1. Cooke had a spider in his ear.
2. Bruce Cooke is frightened of spiders.
3. The spiders stayed in the town for more than 24 hours.
4. Spiders have a way of "flying" in the wind.
5. Rains of spiders do not often happen in Australia.

3 Read the article again quickly and write down eight key words. Retell the story using your key words.

4 Talk about an unusual day. Follow these guidelines.

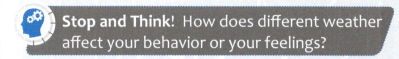

- the wettest day you can remember
- the coldest day in your life
- the hottest day in your community
- a day with a lot of wind or fog
- a terrible storm you remember

- Choose a topic from the list.
- Try to give as many details as possible.
- Speak for five minutes or more.
- Give enough information to answer questions about who, how, what, why, when, where and how long.

Stop and Think! How does different weather affect your behavior or your feelings?

Culture

1 🎧 ²⁵ Read and guess which two facts are false. Then listen and check.

Eight Things You Didn't Know About... Switzerland

1. The capital city of Switzerland is Zurich.
2. Switzerland and the Vatican City are the only countries in the world with square flags.
3. Mont Blanc, Europe's highest mountain, is in Switzerland.
4. Switzerland's **currency** is the euro.
5. Emmental, Swiss cheese, is famous because it has lots of **holes**.
6. Switzerland has four official languages: French, German, Italian and a local language called Romansh.
7. Switzerland is always neutral in wars.
8. The **headquarters** of the Olympic Games are in Switzerland.

2 Read the blog introduction quickly and complete the sentences. Then answer the question.

1. Nicole was born in _____. She's _____.
2. She _____ in the US for five years.
3. She is living in _____ in _____.
4. What does she mean by "I'm going to have to learn to live here all over again"?
   _____

| Home | About | Favorite Pics | Blog |

Beautiful Switzerland
Experiences and anecdotes about my country

Coming Back Home
October 21, by Nicole Baumgartner

So I'm back in my hometown of St. Gallen, Switzerland after living in the United States for the last five years. In the beginning, I was just so pleased to be home, but now I realize I'm going to have to learn to live here all over again.

Life is very different. Swiss people are incredibly **punctual**. If you have a party at 8.00 p.m, everyone arrives on time. Nobody is ever late. It's a disaster for my parents. They're often still preparing food when our visitors **knock** on the door!

The trains and buses are also always on time. If the **timetable** says the bus leaves at 13:43, it leaves at exactly 13:43. I often arrive at the station a minute or two late, and I always see my train leaving.

How do we do it?

It's very simple. In Switzerland, we have very accurate timetables. They use computers to monitor the buses and the trains and if one is often a bit late or a bit early, they **tweak** the timetable.

There are also some very unusual things we do. For example, everyone has their coffee **break** and lunch at exactly the same time. It's not just in school, but in offices, too. So at 9 a.m., 12 p.m. and 4 p.m, there is always big line in coffee shops because everyone wants a coffee at the same time. Why can't people go at different times? I don't understand it!

It's so frustrating! The experts call it "reverse culture shock." My home country feels like a foreign land!

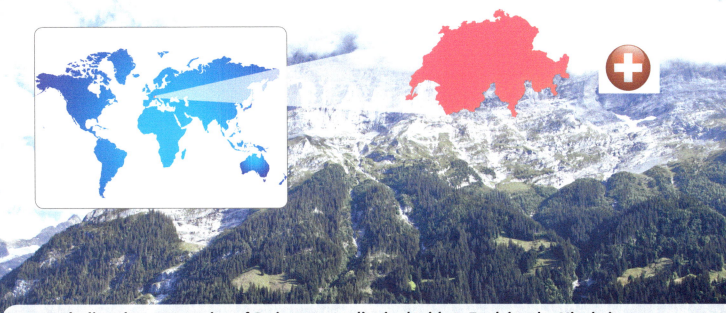

3 Underline three examples of Swiss punctuality in the blog. Explain why Nicole is not happy about them.

4 Complete the definitions using the highlighted words in the blog.
1. information about when public transportation arrives and leaves _____
2. a time when people stop working to relax _____
3. on time, at the right time _____
4. make a loud noise on wood with your hand _____
5. make small changes to something _____

5 Mark (✓) the sentences that are true for you. Are you like people in Switzerland?
1. ☐ I am never late for class.
2. ☐ If I meet my friends, I'm usually the first person to arrive.
3. ☐ I often miss the bus or the train because I'm late.
4. ☐ I sometimes make plans and arrange times, but I sometimes forget about them.
5. ☐ I don't keep a diary or have a calendar.
6. ☐ I don't mind if people are late when I meet them. I'm happy to wait.

6 Write a comment to Nicole's blog about punctuality where you live. Choose one of these situations.
1. the start of classes
2. arriving at parties
3. meeting friends
4. breakfast time, lunch time and dinner time
5. trains and buses

 Stop and Think! Is punctuality important in your culture? When is it most important to be on time?

Glossary
currency: the type of money in a country
hole: a space where there is nothing
headquarters: the most important office of a business or company

105

Project

1 Look at the poster. Answer the questions.
 1. What does the poster mean?
 2. Do you "keep calm and carry on"?
 3. How do you organize yourself when you have a lot of homework to do?
 4. How difficult is it to organize your time?

2 Match the problems with the suggestions. Which one is the most useful for you?
 1. ☐ I have so many things to do that I don't know where to start.
 2. ☐ I have a lot of homework! Should I quit playing basketball?
 3. ☐ I'm always busy! I have extracurricular classes every night. What can I do?
 4. ☐ I'm exhausted and I don't feel like studying. What should I do?
 5. ☐ Classes start so early and I have no time to eat.

 a. No matter what, you should always have breakfast.
 b. You should make a list, prioritize it and follow your agenda.
 c. No, you shouldn't. Exercise helps you relax and keeps you healthy.
 d. That's way too much. You should **cut back**. You need some **downtime**.
 e. You should eat a balanced diet and make sure you get enough rest.

3 Summarize the suggestions in Activity 2 and place them in the corresponding posters on page 107. Use three words maximum.

4 Read and make suggestions using *should*.
 1. What should I do to improve my listening in English?
 _____
 2. What extracurricular activity should I do?
 _____
 3. Should I take my phone to school?
 _____
 4. What should I eat at school?
 _____

5 Make a poster. Follow these guidelines.
- Choose and summarize two suggestions from Activity 4.
- Think of an original background design for your poster.
- Check that your suggestions and the design are thematically related.
- Prepare your posters.

Glossary

cut back: to reduce, to do less

downtime: time when you relax and do not do much

Review

1 Match the sentence parts.

1. ☐ There's a lot of snow today, so
2. ☐ They say it'll rain this afternoon, so
3. ☐ I couldn't sleep last night because
4. ☐ I wanted to take a picture of a plane,
5. ☐ There is heavy fog this morning and
6. ☐ It's very hot today because
7. ☐ We can't play tennis today because

a. but it went into a cloud.
b. it's so windy.
c. it's perfect for skiing.
d. it's very sunny.
e. of the noise from the storm.
f. you can't see very far.
g. take an umbrella to school.

2 Look at the icons and complete using adjectives.

1. We had _____ weather on the ferry. The boat rocked all night!
2. People think London is always _____, but it's not true.
3. It's _____ today, so it's not a good day to go to the beach.
4. It's a _____ day. Let's take photos of the animals at the zoo.
5. The weather forecast said it will be _____ this morning and dry in the afternoon.
6. Close the windows! It's a _____ day today.
7. We always have _____ weather where I live. Perfect weather to make a snowman!

3 Circle the correct options to complete the conversation.

Joe: Hi, Mom. In school, we learned that there are volcanoes in our state.
(1) **Do / Will** we have a volcanic eruption one day?
Mom: No, it (2) **isn't / won't** happen.
Joe: But some volcanoes are live. There (3) **was / will be** a volcanic eruption one day.
Mom: Yes, but it (4) **doesn't / won't** be tomorrow or next week.
Joe: But it is possible!
Mom: Look, when there's an eruption, the government will (5) **give / giving** people information and help. There's nothing to worry about.
Joe: Are you sure?

Mom: I'm sure about one thing, Joe. You (6) **won't / don't** finish your homework tonight because you are worried about volcanoes!

4 Complete the conversation using future with *going to*.

Sharon: Dad, what (1) _____ we _____ (*do*) this summer?

Dad: (2) We _____ (*drive*) across the country in our car.

Frank: Cool! How long (3) _____ we _____ (*travel*)?

Dad: Two weeks. Look. Here's the map. I (4) _____ (*show*) you the route. We _____ (*start*) here in LA.

Sharon: (5) _____ the trip _____ (*end*) in New York?

Dad: No, it isn't. We (6) _____ (*not/visit*) New York. Our final destination is Washington DC, the capital.

Frank: Awesome! (7) _____ I _____ (*see*) the desert?

Dad: Yes, you are. (8) We _____ (*spend*) two days in the desert. Mom (9) _____ (*drive*) there. She loves the desert.

Sharon: Uh… Dad, (10) _____ we _____ (*sleep*) in the car?

Dad: No. We have reservations at hotels across the country.

5 Circle one mistake in each sentence. Then rewrite the sentences.

1. How many people will coming to the party?
   _____

2. It doesn't snow tomorrow.
   _____

3. My brother is go to learn to drive next week.
   _____

4. Are I going to be in your class next year?
   _____

5. Sally don't going to go on the school trip tomorrow.
   _____

6. Do we will have any exams next year?
   _____

6 Complete the agenda, using your own information.

Time	Weather	My plan
Tonight	It will rain.	I'm going to stay at home.
On Friday night		
On Saturday		
Next week		

1 Look and match.

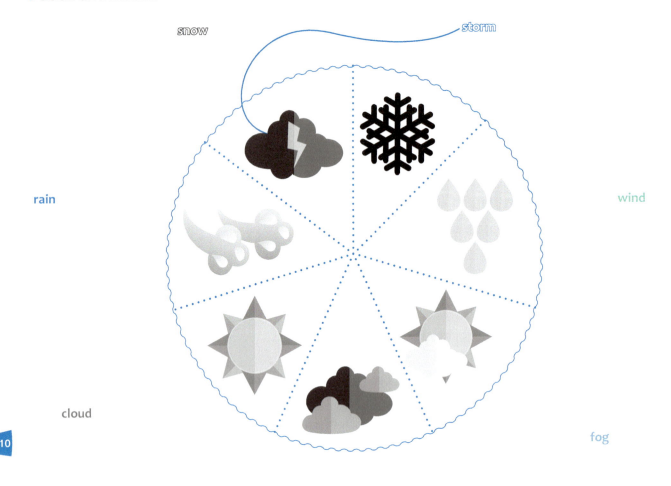

2 Solve the spiral puzzle by writing the adjective forms of the words below.

1. snow
2. wind
3. fog
4. sun
5. rain
6. storm
7. cloud

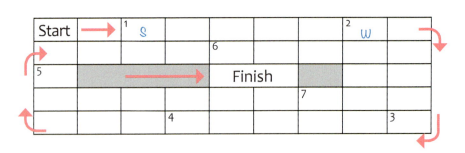

3 Answer the riddles.

1. What goes up when the rain comes down?
2. Why is it cold at Christmas?
3. When does it rain money?
4. What never gets any wetter?
5. What type of bow can't be tied?

a. A rainbow.
b. An ocean.
c. An umbrella.
d. It's Decembrrrr!
e. When there's change in the weather.

Vocabulary

1 🎧26 Listen and repeat the words.

2 🎧27 Listen and complete the sentences.

3 Complete the sentences with the feelings from Activity 1.

Guess What!
When you are very embarrassed, you "turn red."
When you are very frightened, you "turn white."

1. I'm _____ of my sister. She has her own bedroom, but I have to share with my little brother!
2. I'm _____ with my brother because he broke my phone.
3. I sent a photo of my pet rabbit to my best friend, but I also accidentally sent it to everyone in my class. I was so _____! I turned red!
4. They were _____ by that horror movie. They turned white!
5. I'm _____ about my exams. I don't think I will pass all of them.
6. I feel _____ because my hamster died yesterday.
7. I'm always _____ when I'm with my friends. We always laugh together.
8. We're _____ because we're going to be on TV tomorrow! It's amazing!

What did you do on the 4th of July?

1. I made cotton candy! But I was so _____ of my friends—they had fun while I worked!

2. I looked after my dog. The fireworks were very loud and she was _____ of them!

3. I was _____ because there was a party outside my house all night—and I had an exam the next day!

4. Last Independence Day, I dropped an ice cream cone on my T-shirt! I was so _____ my face turned red!

112

4 Write the missing vowels. Then match the adjectives with the noun forms.

Adjective	Noun
1. _ngry	a. fear
2. _mb_rr_ss_d	b. jealousy
3. _xc_t_d	c. anger
4. fr_ght_n_d	d. worry
5. h_ppy	e. happiness
6. j__l__s	f. embarrassment
7. s_d	g. excitement
8. w_rr__d	h. sadness

5 Think Fast! Which feelings are positive? Which are negative?
(3 min)

6 Circle the correct options. Then, in your notebook, rewrite the sentences so they are true for you.

1. In my country, some people get **angry / anger** when they're in traffic.
2. I'm **excited / excitement** because I'm going to see a soccer game on Friday.
3. I'm **frightened / fear** of spiders.
4. My main **worried / worry** at the moment is the school play.
5. I'm terrible at rollerblading. I always feel **embarrassed / embarrassment.**
6. **Happiness / Happy** for me is my family and my cat.

5. Our baseball team played in the state finals. I was so _____—hundreds of people watched the game!

6. I had to sing the national anthem in front of everyone. I was _____ about forgetting the words!

7. My friends and I went swimming in the lake. We were so _____. It was the best day of the year!

8. I always feel _____ on Independence Day because my grandma died on this day three years ago.

113

Grammar

1 Take the quiz.

The Feelings QUIZ!

Why are some people naturally happy but others are **grumpy**? Can we teach ourselves to be happy? Take the quiz and find out!

① **Your schoolwork is stressful. What do you do?**
   a. ☐ I do more work, and I stay up late to finish it.
   b. ☐ I talk to my friends, and I work with them. Maybe they have the same problem.
   c. ☐ I exercise to **take my mind off** it.

② **Your sports team just lost an important game. What did you do?**
   a. ☐ We had a big argument and criticized each other.
   b. ☐ We discussed it as a team, and we agreed to improve next time.
   c. ☐ We didn't mind. We played for fun, not to win.

③ **Do you have a lot of hobbies?**
   a. ☐ No, I just watch TV and play computer games. It's OK.
   b. ☐ Yes, I have some, but I prefer to hang out with my friends.
   c. ☐ Yes, and I want to **make a living** from my hobby one day!

④ **You have a big problem. Who will you ask for help?**
   a. ☐ Nobody. I don't know a lot of people who can help me.
   b. ☐ My best friend or my parents. It depends on the problem!
   c. ☐ Everyone! All my friends will **lend a helping hand**.

⑤ **You see a really funny video on YouTube. Are you going to share it?**
   a. ☐ No, I'm going to laugh to myself, and then write a comment online.
   b. ☐ Yes, I'm going to show it to my friends.
   c. ☐ Yes, and then I'm going to look for another one. I love to laugh!

Check your answers
Mostly A: Uh oh…, you get stressed and angry too easily. Learn to relax. Call a friend. Go out.
Mostly B: You accept life's problems, but you also like the support of your friends when things go wrong. This is a good strategy!
Mostly C: Wow! You are one happy person! You must smile a lot. We're jealous!

 Stop and Think! How important are friends and family in keeping people happy?

Questions

Use this pattern to make most information questions in English.

(Wh– word) + auxiliary + subject + verb + complement?
(Where) does  study English?

2 Complete the sentences with the question words. Then interview a partner.

how   how many   how much   what   when   where

1. _____ people are there in your family?
2. _____ do you live?
3. _____ money do you spend in a day?
4. _____ are you going to do after school today?
5. _____ can I improve my English? Any ideas?
6. _____ did you go on your last vacation?

3 Write questions for the highlighted parts of the sentences.

1. _____
   I'm **from Montana**.
2. _____
   We had a **pizza** in the mall.
3. _____
   I like **ice cream** for dessert.
4. _____
   We usually go to the movies on the **weekend**.
5. _____
   We're waiting for **the bus**.
6. _____
   This afternoon? I'm not sure. I think I'll **go skating**.

Glossary

grumpy: easily angry

take my mind off it: to stop worrying about something, usually by doing something else

make a living: to make money from doing work

lend a helping hand: to help

Which and What

Use *which* when you choose from a number of options.

Which ball would you like?
Use *what* when you have many options.

What would you like to eat?

4 Circle the correct options to complete the sentences.

1. Look at all these suitcases! **What / Which** one is yours?
2. Sorry. **Which / What** is Camilla's last name? I never asked her.
3. So **which / what** girl in this picture is your sister?
4. There's a green, a red and a blue pen. **Which / What** one would you like?
5. Good afternoon. Welcome to the Blue Street Café. **Which / What** would you like?
6. There are three flights to Mexico City! **Which / What** one is ours?

Writing & Speaking

1 Read the movie review quickly. How many stars does the reviewer give *Jurassic World*?

Summary | Critic Review | User Reviews

Jurassic World

Reviewer score
★★★★★

Director: Colin Trevorrow
Writers: Rick Jaffa (screenplay), Amanda Silver (screenplay), 5 more credits »
Stars: Chris Pratt, Bryce Dallas Howard, Ty Simpkins | See full cast and crew

¹ *Jurassic World* is the latest sequel to 1993's *Jurassic Park* and it is monster-sized fun.

² The movie is set on the fictional island of Isla Nubar where scientists brought a new group of dinosaurs back to life. The dinosaurs appear in a kind of **safari park** where they entertain tourists. In the classic *Jurassic Park* style, one of the dinosaurs escapes, and suddenly, everyone is in danger.

³ The plot is predictable, but the movie is never boring. The exciting action keeps on moving for the whole two hours. There are moments of comedy too, especially from the movie's star Chris Pratt. Pratt plays an expert on velociraptors, the most popular dinosaurs from the first movie. He is also responsible for the movie's iconic scene when he faces three velociraptors on his own, with no **weapons** to protect him.

▶ 116

⁴ Also in the cast is Bryce Dallas Howard, the **owner** of the park, as well as B.D. Wong, who is back playing geneticist Dr. Henry Wu from the very first movie.

⁵ There's only one thing most of us want to know: what are the dinosaurs like? The special effects are spectacular. There are swimming, flying and running dinosaurs of all descriptions. The marine mosasaurus is the best of all. It is terrifying.

⁶ *Jurassic World* is a spectacular movie, although some moments might be too frightening for young children. You can't miss this movie.

2 Match the content summaries to the paragraphs in the review. Write the numbers.

☐ an actor who returns to the movie series
☐ the different dinosaurs
☐ who the film is not appropriate for
☐ introduction
☐ the most famous moment of the film
☐ where it happens

Be Strategic!
When reading, think carefully about the content of each paragraph. Write a note about the content next to each paragraph. This will help you write a summary of a text.

3 Read some opinions about Jurassic World. Match them to the correct type of opinion.

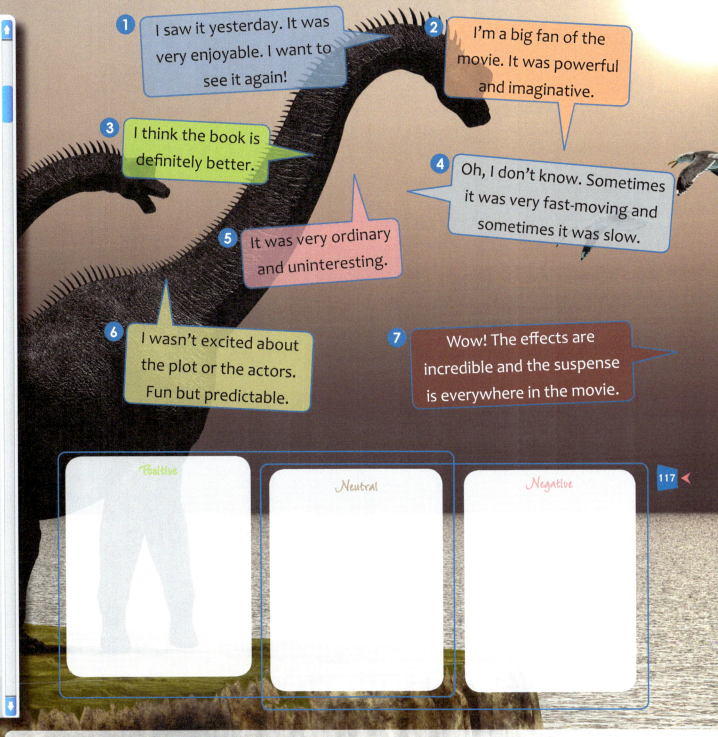

1. I saw it yesterday. It was very enjoyable. I want to see it again!
2. I'm a big fan of the movie. It was powerful and imaginative.
3. I think the book is definitely better.
4. Oh, I don't know. Sometimes it was very fast-moving and sometimes it was slow.
5. It was very ordinary and uninteresting.
6. I wasn't excited about the plot or the actors. Fun but predictable.
7. Wow! The effects are incredible and the suspense is everywhere in the movie.

Positive | Neutral | Negative

4 Write a review about movie you know. Include information about the following:
- the plot
- the cast
- the director
- best scene
- special effects (if there are any)
- who is it for? (the whole family?)

5 Share your reviews in small groups. Decide what movie to see.

Glossary
safari park: a place like a zoo where animals can move freely
weapons: things people use to hunt or kill, like guns or knives
owner: a person who possesses something

Culture

1 🎧²⁸ **Listen and complete the fact file with numbers.**

India is the (1) _____ biggest country in the world. Its population is around (2) _____ billion people. There are (3) _____ official languages—Hindi and English—but there are about (4) _____ languages spoken in India. There are also many different religions. The most common religion is Hinduism. Around (5) _____ % of Indians are Hindus.

2 **Read about the Indian festival of Holi. In your notebook, answer the questions.**

 118

1. Why is Holi similar to January 1ˢᵗ?
2. How many explanations are there for the origin of the festival?
3. What emotion do people celebrate at the festival?
4. How do we know music is an important part of Holi?
5. Do people treat elderly people differently at Holi?
6. What do people look like at the end of the festival?

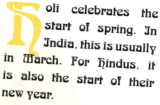

The Hindu Festival of Color

Holi celebrates the start of spring. In India, this is usually in March. For Hindus, it is also the start of their new year.

Holi is a religious festival. It celebrates an event from the life of the god, Krishna. As a boy, Krishna once threw colored water on some girls at a farm. He did this because he was a naughty child.

There is another story, too. At one time, Krishna was jealous of his future wife's beautiful skin. His mother told him to paint his wife's face in any color he wanted. People today paint their faces in extraordinary colors at Holi.

Holi is a time of practical jokes. It is a great celebration of happiness. People dance and sing and throw colored paint and water on their friends, family and passersby. Nobody is safe!

Everyone is invited to play, not just Hindus. Many foreign visitors and tourists join in the fun, but they don't all have clean clothes afterwards!

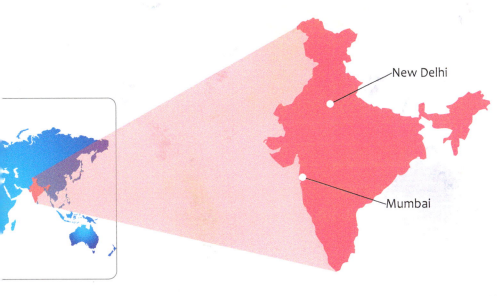

3 In your notebook, rewrite the stories of Krishna using these words. Then compare with a partner.

1. god / Krishna / water / girls / naughty

2. god / Krishna / future wife / mother / face

4 In your notebook, write a short, 50-word reply to this question.

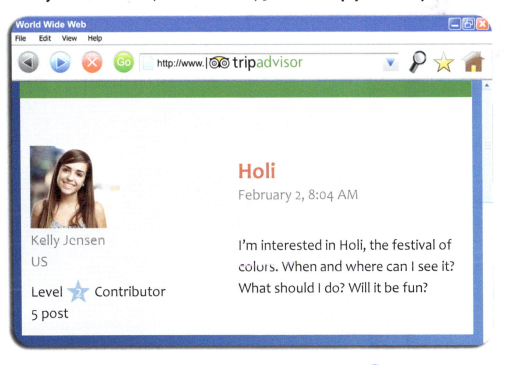

Holi

February 2, 8:04 AM

Kelly Jensen
US

Level ★ Contributor
5 post

I'm interested in Holi, the festival of colors. When and where can I see it? What should I do? Will it be fun?

Stop and Think! Are feelings easy to share with others? Which are?

Glossary

naughty: behaving disobediently

practical jokes: a physical trick you play on people

passersby: people in the street, members of the public

Project

1 Read the brochure about a national holiday. Complete the chart.

Name of national holiday	
Day of celebration	
Reason for celebration	

2 Read the poem in the article. In your notebook, answer the questions.
1. Who is the poet writing to?
2. How does he feel?
3. Why does he mention a rose and a piece of music?

3 Complete the chart about famous people in your country.

musician	poet	writer	painter	sculptor

4 Make a brochure for a national holiday for one of the famous people in the chart. Consider the following information.
- the dates / times of the festival
- the importance of the festival
- the clothes people will wear
- the food people will eat
- other activities people will do during the festival
- pictures that could illustrate the festival

 120

Stop and Think! What does music make you feel? A painting? A poem?

Burns Night

My love is like a red, red rose
That's newly sprung in June:
My love is like the melody
That's sweetly played in tune.

Burns Night is a public holiday in Scotland. It celebrates the life of Scotland's national poet, Robert Burns (1759-1796). It is celebrated on January 25th every year, the anniversary of the poet's birth.
In Burns' time, most writers were rich people from the aristocracy. Burns was special because he came from a poor family.
His poems are beautiful messages of love of people and nature:

On Burns night people get together with their families and friends. Many men often wear kilts, a piece of cloth that they wear around the legs. They usually eat a special meal—haggis—the national dish of Scotland.
It's a day of national pride for Scottish people both at home and around the world.

Review

1 Look at the emoticons and write the nouns. What is the mystery word?

1. 😨
2. 😊
3. 😠
4. 😃
5. 🙂
6. 😟
7. 😣
8. 😢

2 Complete the chart with the words below.

angry   embarrassed   excited   frightened   happy   jealous   sad   worried

Positive Adjectives	Negative Adjectives

3 Circle the correct options to complete the story.

My friends bought Josie and me a present. It was a bungee jump. Josie was (1) **excited / excitement**. She really wanted to do it and I was (2) **jealous / jealousy** of her. I had this terrible feeling of (3) **frightened / fear** and she didn't. My (4) **worried / worry** was safety: is a bungee jump 100% safe?
When we got there, I didn't want to move. My face turned red with (5) **embarrassed / embarrassment**. Thankfully, the other people weren't (6) **angry / anger**. In fact, they were very patient.
My friends were there and I didn't want them to feel (7) **sad / sadness** because they paid for the wrong present. So, yes, I did it! I jumped! The wind was in my hair and the ground came closer and closer… and then finally it stopped!
In the end, I had this amazing feeling of (8) **happy / happiness**. I was alive! I survived! I laughed and laughed and laughed, but I will never, ever do it again!

122

4 Complete the questions using the words below.

how   how long   how much   what   when   where   who   why

1. A: _____ did you stay at the youth hostel?
   B: Three days.
2. A: _____ is this sandwich?
   B: It's $5.
3. A: _____ did you see at the party?
   B: Anna, George and Tony.
4. A: _____ are you looking at your phone?
   B: I'm waiting for an important message.
5. A: _____ is your favorite food?
   B: Nachos with cheese. I love them!
6. A: _____ time do you go to bed?
   B: About 10:30 every night.
7. A: _____ is your apartment?
   B: We live on Central Avenue above the supermarket.
8. A: _____ do you play chess?
   B: It's easy! I'll teach you.

5 Complete the questions with auxiliary verbs. Write one word in each blank.

1. A: What _____ you usually do on weekends?
   B: We go to our theater group on Saturdays and have a family dinner on Sunday.
2. A: What _____ the weather be like tomorrow?
   B: Foggy in the morning and cloudy in the afternoon.
3. A: _____ you enjoy the movie yesterday?
   B: Yes! It was great.
4. A: _____ you have to study Spanish at your school?
   B: Yes, it's compulsory.
5. A: Where _____ your sister going to go on vacation?
   B: To Machu Picchu in Peru!
6. A: How _____ you feeling today?
   B: Terrible! I have a cold.
7. A: Where _____ your grandparents live?
   B: In Santiago, Chile.
8. A: _____ you swim?
   B: No, I can't, but I want to learn.

6 Circle the correct options.

1. There are sixteen classrooms in the school. **Which / What** one is yours?
2. **Which / What** door is my doctor's office?
3. **Which / What** is the freezing temperature of water?
4. My mom's a manager. **Which / What** does your mom do?
5. **Which / What** gate does our flight leave from: 47A or 47B?
6. **Which / What** does *embarrassed* mean in English?
7. These pictures are by all the students in our class. **Which / What** is your favorite?
8. I usually play soccer on the weekend. **Which / What** do you usually do?

1 **Unscramble the feelings. Then use the numbered letters to find the mystery feeling.**

l e s o j u a

a d s

r e d w o i r

b r a s s e r m a d e

y a p h p

g r a n y

t e x c i e d

g r e e n f i t h d

Mystery feeling

2 **Find the extra word in each sentence. Then unscramble the words to form a question.**

1. They will go to the movies will this weekend.
2. What she ate eggs and toast for breakfast.
3. He's going to play soccer this tomorrow.
4. She do practices the piano every day.
5. You your sister is going to hang out with friends.
6. It's late! We want pizza for dinner afternoon.

Mystery question

3 **What am I?**

You will see nothing else when you look me in the face. I will look you in the eye and I will never lie.

Workbook

Unit 1

Vocabulary – School Supplies

1 Look and label the pictures.

- calculator
- dictionary
- eraser
- gym uniform
- pen
- pencil
- recorder
- ruler
- sneakers

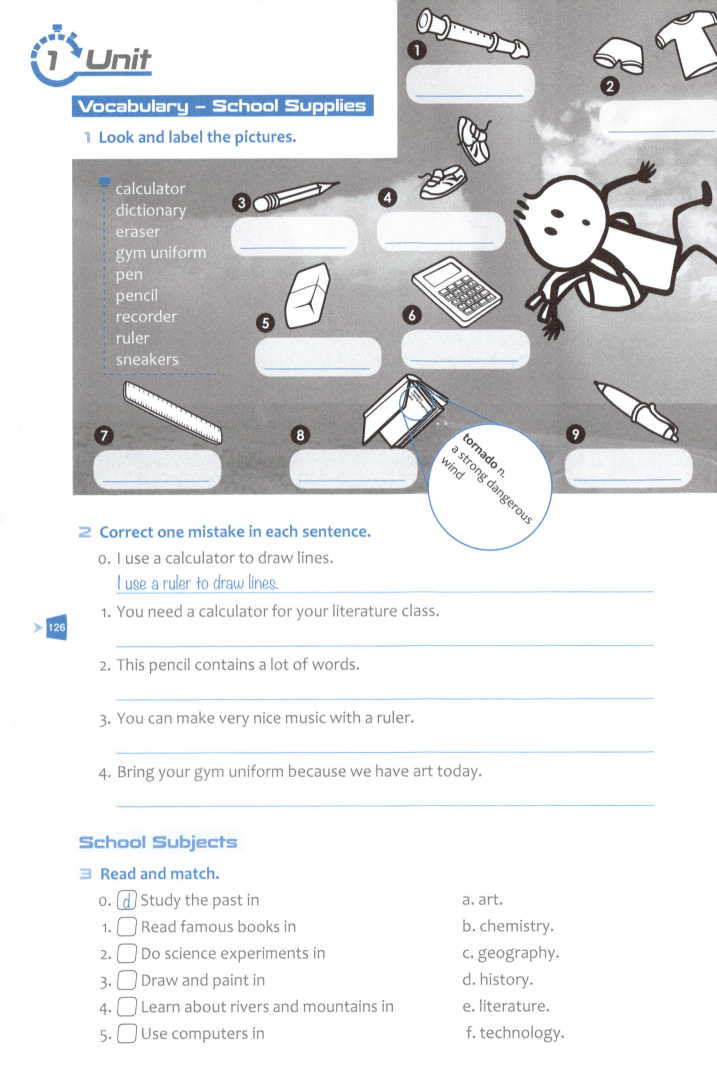

tornado n. a strong dangerous wind

2 Correct one mistake in each sentence.

0. I use a calculator to draw lines.
   I use a ruler to draw lines.

1. You need a calculator for your literature class.
   _____

2. This pencil contains a lot of words.
   _____

3. You can make very nice music with a ruler.
   _____

4. Bring your gym uniform because we have art today.
   _____

School Subjects

3 Read and match.

0. [d] Study the past in   a. art.
1. [ ] Read famous books in   b. chemistry.
2. [ ] Do science experiments in   c. geography.
3. [ ] Draw and paint in   d. history.
4. [ ] Learn about rivers and mountains in   e. literature.
5. [ ] Use computers in   f. technology.

4 **Read and complete the text.**

Sammy Bloom

3 hours ago -

I'm very lucky because I live in the countryside. This is my horse Mr. Barley. I always give Mr. Barley his breakfast (0) __in__ the morning before school. He lives on a farm. When I'm at school (1) _____ the afternoon, he is outside with the other horses. He has an easy life! I come home (2) _____ the evening and we go riding. (3) _____ night, he sleeps in the stable (that's where horses live). Mr. Barley is my favorite horse!

Like Comment Share

Spelling

Some verbs need spelling changes in present simple.

c + y: stud*y* → stud*ies*
v + y: pl*ay* → pl*ays*
e: driv*e* → driv*es*
o: g*o* → g*oes*

c = consonant   v = vowel

Grammar – Present Simple

1 **Look and circle the correct option.**

0. We **like** / **likes** literature.
1. Ian **has** / **have** a cool phone.
2. Peter **studies** / **study** at 11:30 every day.
3. My parents **drive** / **drives** the same car.
4. Carl **go** / **goes** to school on the bus every day.
5. You **speak** / **speaks** very good English.
6. Rachel **do** / **does** her homework at the library.

2 **Make negative sentences.**

0. My grandparents live with us.
   My grandparents don't live with us.

1. I want a dog.
   _____

2. My mom drives the school bus.
   _____

3. Melanie has your ruler.
   _____

4. They speak Japanese.
   _____

5. You play soccer in the afternoon.
   _____

Unit 1

3 Read and complete the conversation with *do* or *does*.

3:34 PM
Grandpa, (0) *do* you go to the gym every day?

3:38 PM
Yes, I (1) _____!

3:41 PM
What exercises (2) _____ you do?

3:42 PM
Running, swimming and weights! I'm retired so I (3) _____ work. I have lots of time.

3:42 PM
(4) _____ grandma come to the gym with you?

3:47 PM
No, she (5) _____. She's always on her motorcycle.

3:49 PM
What? (6) _____ grandma drive a motorcycle?

3:51 PM
Yes, she (7) _____. She drives really fast!

4 Read and complete the sentences.

always ~~often~~ never sometimes usually

0. My photo is ____*often*____ on the school Facebook page. It's there once a week.
1. I _____ see my cousins. Maybe once or twice a year.
2. We _____ bike to school every day, but today we're on the bus.
3. School is _____ closed on Sunday.
4. My sister is allergic to bread, so she _____ eats it.

Guess What!
once → one time
twice → two times

Review

1 Complete about you!

1. I never _____ in the morning.
2. I sometimes _____ in the evening.
3. I often _____ before school.
4. I always _____ at night.
5. I usually _____ on the weekend.

Reading

1 Read and circle T (True) or F (False).

1. Johnny's village is in a valley. T F
2. Johnny goes to school in a car. T F
3. The children in Johnny's school wear the same clothes. T F
4. Johnny usually arrives late. T F
5. Students want to become professionals. T F
6. Many successful athletes come from Johnny's country. T F

Marathon Journey to School
Megan Skoles

"The discipline these children have to attend school helps them follow their dreams."

Going to school is not always easy for many young people. Many students have very difficult journeys to school every day. One student is Johnny from Kenya. He lives in the mountains with his parents and his younger sister. His village doesn't have a school bus and no one has a car. So he walks five kilometers to school every morning. Many children come from poor families and often walk to school in bare feet. In Johnny's community, shoes are optional, but a uniform is mandatory in elementary school. Students wear brown shorts, red sweaters and blue shirts.

The journey to school is long and hard, but Johnny is always on time. He usually walks, but he often runs.

The discipline these children have to attend school helps them follow their dreams. Some have goals of becoming professionals to help their communities or pilots to travel around the world. Others are inspired to become professional athletes and their chances are good! Many of the best long-distance runners in the world come from Kenya.

Johnny in class (far right).

Writing

2 Look and write the times using the words.

o'clock past to

0. It's quarter to two.
1. _____
2. _____
3. _____
4. _____
5. _____

3 Read the article again and rewrite it from Johnny's point of view.

My name's Johnny. I'm from Kenya. _____
_____
_____
_____

Unit 2

Vocabulary – Jobs

1 Look and complete the jobs.

0. h <u>a i r</u> s t y <u>l i s</u> t
1. r e c _ _ t _ _ n _ _ t
2. f _ r e _ i g _ t _ _
3. t _ a _ _ i t o _ e _ _ t _ r
4. e _ g _ n _ e r
5. p _ _ _ t

Workplaces

2 Find and write five workplaces.

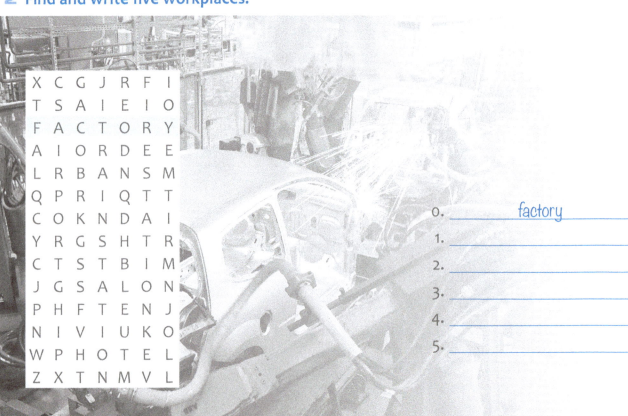

```
X C G J R F I
T S A I E I O
F A C T O R Y
A I O R D E E
L R B A N S M
Q P R I Q T T
C O K N D A I
Y R G S H T R
C T S T B I M
J G S A L O N
P H F T E N J
N I V I U K O
W P H O T E L
Z X T N M V L
```

0. factory
1. _____
2. _____
3. _____
4. _____
5. _____

3 Choose the correct option.

airport factory hotel train station fire station salon

0. Arrive at the _____airport_____ two hours before your flight.
1. I want a new hairstyle. I need to go to the _____.
2. My dad works in a _____. They make plasma TVs.
3. Trains leave early morning from the central _____.
4. We're staying in a nice _____ for our vacation.
5. You can see the red trucks at the _____.

Grammar – Present Continuous

Spelling

Double the final consonant in verbs that have a c + v + c combination.

r u n → ru **n n** ing
st e p → ste **p p** ing
j o g → jo **g g** ing

c = consonant   v = vowel

1 Look at the pictures. What are they doing?

0. (snowboard) He's snowboarding.
1. (sing) _____
2. (wait) _____
3. (cook) _____
4. (read) _____

2 Complete the sentences with the present continuous.

~~have~~ make run sing swim write

0. She _'s having_ lunch with her cousins.
1. Right now I _____ an e-mail to my friends.
2. Zara _____ in the sea.
3. The boys _____ a model of a ship in their bedroom.
4. Alice and Petra _____ in the marathon!
5. The soprano _____ an opera.

Unit 2

Review

1 Write sentences. What are they doing?

0. I <u>am studying English.</u>
1. My mom _____
2. My teacher _____
3. My cousins _____
4. My best friend _____

Reading

1 Look at the title of the article. Guess the topic.

1. ☐ fishing 2. ☐ science 3. ☐ tourism

Strange Jobs

The Whale Watcher

By Claire Rhine

> 132

Dr. Lola Friend is sitting on a boat in the Indian Ocean. The day is calm and it's very hot. Nobody is speaking. Suddenly, she is jumping up and shouting. "A blow! A blow!"

Immediately, we're moving across the sea where there is still some **spray** in the air. We are looking for the world's largest animal, the blue whale, and there's one right in front of us!

It's swimming next to the boat and it is enormous.

Lola is a marine biologist. She's a doctor of zoology and she studies whales in her job.

"For many people, it's a dream job," she explains. "Lots of people want to work with animals and protect the environment."

But are there any **downsides** to the job?

"Sure," she laughs, "it's not easy to see whales. They are not common and they spend most of their time under the water. We often spend days on the boat and we see nothing. You just sit and look at the sea. Nothing changes. It's like a blue desert!"

But today we're chasing a **huge** whale and it is a spectacular sight to see!

2 Read the article and circle T (True) or F (False).

1. Dr. Friend works in a hospital.   T   F
2. They are in the Pacific.   T   F
3. They are having a successful day.   T   F
4. Many people want to do Dr. Friend's job.   T   F
5. Dr. Friend sees blue whales all the time.   T   F
6. Dr. Friend loves to sit and look at the sea.   T   F

Writing

1 Circle 10 spelling mistakes. Then correct them.

Dear Janet,

(Tank) you for your e-mail about my job as a marine biologist. Here are the answers too your questions.

I like my job because I work whit animals. Whales are so beautyful. They are wonderful.

In general, I spend a lot of tyme at sea. Research is a very imporant part of our work. Sometimes I'm away from home for meny weeks and I miss my family. I miss eating at hom.

At the momen, I'm spending a month in Sri Lanka. It's a grate experience.

Thanks once again for you e-mail.

Regards,

Lola

0. _____Thank_____
1. _____
2. _____
3. _____
4. _____
5. _____
6. _____
7. _____
8. _____
9. _____
10. _____

2 Choose a job and write an e-mail to Janet in your notebook.

zookeeper

window washer

Glossary

spray: small drops of water in the air

downsides: disadvantages of a situation

huge: extremely big

Unit 3

Vocabulary – Clothes

1 Unscramble the words and find them in the word search.

0. aoct ____coat____
1. essdr _____
2. tha _____
3. sejna _____
4. fsrac _____

5. shtsro _____
6. skneesar _____
7. cosks _____
8. setware _____

```
S F K E W M H G X D S
O W M S C A G W C R R
C G E C T M H E E T V
K J E A N S X K T D T
S H O R T S A D J X W
S C W F P E M M L T N
X R S Z N R R R Z F K
X H R S L D Y U H E I
```

Guess What!
There are different materials to make clothes:
leather   wool   cotton

2 Cross out the the word that doesn't belong. Explain why it's different.

0. belt / ~~sweater~~ / shoes   _A belt and shoes are made of leather._
1. jeans / scarf / sweater   _____
2. blouse / hat / T-shirt   _____
3. jeans / pants / sneakers   _____
4. coat / scarf / shorts   _____
5. jeans / socks / sneakers   _____

134

3 Look and complete with as many clothes words as you can.

1. Zack is wearing _____

2. Louise is wearing _____

Grammar – Comparatives

Spelling

Adjectives with a c + v + c combination.
b i g → bi **gg** er → the bi **gg** est
th i n → thi **nn** er → the thi **nn** est

Note:
good → better → the best
bad → worse → the worst
far → farther → the farthest

c = consonant   v = vowel

1 Complete the sentences with the comparative form of the adjectives.

0. Dogs are _____better_____ (good) friends than cats.
1. Your apartment is _____ (big) than mine.
2. August is _____ (hot) than July in my country.
3. The train station is _____ (far) than the bus station.
4. My Spanish is _____ (bad) than my Portuguese.
5. My biology book is _____ (thin) than my dictionary.

2 Correct one mistake in each sentence.

0. The main square is prettyer than the town square.
   The main square is prettier than the town square.
1. The mall is more far than the school.

2. A horse is more fast than a dog.

3. Your suitcase is heavyer than my bag.

4. Yoga is more good than swimming.

5. You're intelligenter than him!

Unit 3

Superlatives

3 Unscramble the superlative sentences in your notebook.

0. buildings in / The pyramids / Egypt. / are / the oldest
   <u>The pyramids are the oldest buildings in Egypt.</u>
1. on the planet. / Tokyo / the largest / city / is
2. is / Solar System. / Jupiter / the biggest / planet / in the
3. successful / *Avatar* / the most / movie / of all time. / is
4. on the planet. / Mount Everest / mountain / is / the highest
5. on Earth. / is / the most / Malaria / disease / dangerous
6. woman / The world's / tall. / shortest / is / 0.62 meters

4 Rewrite the sentences using the superlative.

0. I'm taller than the other students in my class.
   <u>I'm the tallest student in my class.</u>
1. Our classroom is larger than the other classrooms in the school.

2. My little brother is younger than the other kids in his kindergarten.

3. The hot chocolate is more expensive than the other drinks in the restaurant.

4. Monday is busier than the other days in school.

5. March is wetter than the other months.

6. The stormtrooper costume is better than the other costumes.

Review

1 Complete about you.

1. I'm the best in my class at _____.
2. I'm younger than _____.
3. I'm taller than _____.
4. My worst school subject is _____.
5. My country is hotter than _____.
6. The oldest person in my family is _____.

Reading

1 Read the text quickly (skimming) and mark (✓) the correct topic.

1. ☐ traditions
2. ☐ breakfast
3. ☐ cooking

Breakfast around the World

Bzzz ... the alarm clock rings and everyone gets up. But does everyone eat the same breakfast all around the world? Absolutely not!

England

The full English breakfast is the largest breakfast in our selection. It's all fried food: fried eggs, bacon, sausages, mushrooms... and even fried bread. It's also served with beans and tomatoes. It has lots of **calories** so you can't eat it every day. And to drink? This is England, so you drink tea with milk, of course!

The Philippines

The most popular breakfast in the Philippines is called *tapsilog*. It contains rice with an egg and also some dried meat, for example, chicken. It's the perfect start to a busy day because it gives you **plenty** of energy.

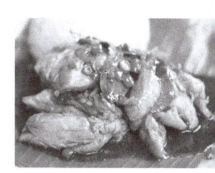

Pakistan

In Pakistan, people like to have something hot to start the day. The classic breakfast is called *nihari*. It is a beef or lamb **curry** which you eat with a local bread called a *naan*. It's the hottest breakfast on our world tour!

2 Read and find (scanning) one breakfast...

1. for an athlete. _____
2. which is spicy. _____
3. which has a lot of fat. _____

3 Read again and circle T (True) or F (False).

1. All breakfasts include something to drink.   T   F
2. The English breakfast can make people fat.   T   F
3. People in the Philippines eat chicken for breakfast.   T   F
4. Nihari is extremely spicy.   T   F

Writing

4 Describe a breakfast in your country or in your family.

_____
_____

Glossary

calorie: a measure of energy in food

plenty: as much as necessary

curry: a type of food made from vegetables, meat and spices

Vocabulary – Food

1 Find and write seven types of food.

O R A N G E V L Y P
A R Y V V H L I O O
P Q J J D U E M N T
P Y Z X D W T E I A
L C A R R O T Z O T
E P T F K U U J N O
O Q X H V Z C T H Q
S T R A W B E R R Y

0. _orange_   4. _____
1. _____   5. _____
2. _____   6. _____
3. _____   7. _____

2 Guess what fruit or vegetable each picture suggests.

0. potatoes

3 Match the parts of the sentences.

0. [c] Plants need nutrients, so give them some
1. [ ] The garden is very dry, so I'm
2. [ ] Mom wants some flowers, so let's plant some
3. [ ] The carrots are ready, so Dad's
4. [ ] These earthworms are
5. [ ] All the fruit is ready, so we're
6. [ ] The snails and caterpillars are
7. [ ] There are no vegetables in the garden—only

a. seeds.
b. good for the garden.
c. fertilizer.
d. eating all my lettuces!
e. watering it.
f. weeds.
g. picking it.
h. digging them out.

4 **Correct the false information in the sentences.**

0. Earthworms become butterflies.
   Caterpillars become butterflies.

1. You dig oranges out of the ground.
   _____

2. Potatoes have seeds.
   _____

3. You give fertilizer to dogs.
   _____

4. You pick carrots off a tree.
   _____

5. Snails move very fast in the garden.
   _____

6. Earthworms live in trees.
   _____

Grammar – Countable and Uncountable Nouns

1 **Complete the questions with *much* or *many*.**

0. How ___much___ sugar do you eat?
1. How _____ apples are there in the fridge?
2. How _____ water do you drink every day?
3. How _____ bags do you usually take to school?
4. How _____ eggs do you need to make a cake?
5. How _____ milk do you drink a week?

2 **Choose the correct option for each picture.**

0. ☐ a few eggs
   ☑ a lot of eggs

1. ☐ a little sugar
   ☐ a lot of sugar

2. ☐ a lot of chocolate
   ☐ some chocolate

3. ☐ a few ice cream
   ☐ a little ice cream

4. ☐ some meat
   ☐ a few meat

5. ☐ a few tea
   ☐ some tea

Unit 4

The Chicago Werewolf!

3 Choose the correct option to complete the newspaper story.

It happens every night: I wake up and I see (0) **a few / a lot of** garbage in our front yard. It happens at (1) **a few / a little** houses in our neighborhood. In the morning, people often see (2) **some / any** apples in the street or (3) **some / any** eggs in the road. What is opening the trash at night?
Our neighbors think there are (4) **some / any** wild animals in our street, but we live in Chicago—in the middle of the city.
The newspaper calls it *The Chicago Werewolf*. Of course, there aren't (5) **any / some** monsters here. So what is happening?
I think I know. There are (6) **a lot of / much** coyotes in Chicago. They look like dogs, so that's why people think it's a werewolf. There's only (7) **a few / a little** food for them in the city. That's why they open the trash cans at night. They want to find (8) **a few / a little** sausages to eat or (9) **a few / a little** bacon for their breakfast.

Guess What!
Besides food, many other things are countable (boys, cats, books, etc.) and uncountable (information, air, music, etc.).

Review

1 Look at the picture. What is in the fridge?

0. (coffee) _There isn't any coffee._
1. (bananas) _____
2. (strawberries) _____
3. (cheese) _____
4. (milk) _____
5. (apples) _____
6. (water) _____
7. (carrots) _____

Glossary

werewolf: an imaginary creature that turns into a wolf in the full moon

sausage: a mixture of meat and spices in a long tube

bacon: meat from a pig in long thin slices

Reading

1 Read the blog and mark (✓) three differences in the original plan.

> The Animals in My Country
> Paragraph 1: About me
> Paragraph 2: A mammal from Puerto Rico
> Paragraph 3: A famous fish from Puerto Rico
> Paragraph 4: A bird from Puerto Rico
> Paragraph 5: A scary snake from Puerto Rico
> Final paragraph 6: Conclusion

The Animals in My Country

My country is Puerto Rico. It is part of the United States, but it isn't actually a state. It is a group of islands with mountains and rainforests. Puerto Rico is the habitat of many different animals.

There are many mammals in my country. The most common are bats. We have thirteen different species of them. They are very good because they eat mosquitoes.

The most amazing animals in Puerto Rico are the manatees. They are shy animals that live in the sea and they are very fat. They look a bit like whales. Manatees are an endangered species.

Like many Caribbean countries, Puerto Rico has lots of birds. One of the most famous is the Puerto Rican parrot. It has green feathers and a red face. It is also an endangered species. It is possible that there are only 80 birds now in the country.

In conclusion, Puerto Rico has a lot of different animals, but many of them are in danger. It is important for everyone to work hard to protect our environment and save these species.

2 Correct the false information in the sentences.

0. Puerto Rico is part of Mexico, but it is not a state.
   Puerto Rico is part of the US, but it is not a state.

1. There are 13 types of birds in Puerto Rico.
   _____

2. Bats eat the island's dogs.
   _____

3. Manatees are large insects.
   _____

4. The red and green Puerto Rican butterfly is an endangered species.
   _____

Writing

1 Write a similar blog. Follow this plan:

- Research animals from your country on the Internet.
- Choose three famous animals.
- Write one paragraph about each one.
- Describe what the animals eat.
- Describe their appearance.
- Describe where they live.
- Write an interesting introduction and a conclusion.

Unit 5

Vocabulary – Pastimes

1 Unscramble the words to complete the post.

Juana Echeverry. February 10

Top Tips for Surviving a Rainy Day

It's raining and you don't know what to do. You can forget about popping a (0) __wheelie__ (*ilheewe*) in the park or going (1) _____ (*rollingerdlba*) with your buddies. I live in Quibdo, in Colombia. It's the wettest place in South America! Some suggestions:

- Play a (2) _____ (*orbad*) game like Monopoly or Clue. It's much more fun to do things with your family.

- Make a (3) _____ (*lomed*). It's easy to do and you can get kits online.

- Find your pencils and do some (4) _____ (*wardgin*). Have competitions on different themes: a zoo animal, a dinosaur, whatever you like!

- Do something active like (5) _____ (*canngid*) at home. Yes! Get a training video from the Internet and learn the moves to the music.

- Don't be shy to call a friend. You can use a program like Skype to chat with lots of friends at the same time—it's like (6) _____ (*gangnih*) out when you're in town. You need this when you're trapped at home (it happens a lot in Quibdo!).

What are your top tips for a rainy day?

Roy Jones Thanks these are great suggestions. I live in London and it's very rainy here.
Saturday at 10:05 am via mobile . Like

Marian Kiev These are really good ideas!
Sunday at 5:25 pm via mobile . Like

2 Look and complete the sentences.

0. We're __camping__ this weekend.
1. Eric's _____ in front of his friends.
2. Simon is _____ in the pool.
3. Let's _____ this afternoon.
4. I love _____ pictures of aliens and ships.
5. I enjoy _____ at the park on weekends.
6. He's _____ to some cool music.

3 Match the pieces to make sentences.

0. Get out of the pool! Joe's doing —— a. drawing landscapes.
1. My friends and I hang   b. a model of the Empire State building.
2. Next vacation, I want to go   —c. a cannonball.
3. Look at this picture. Danny loves   d. out at the café.
4. Beth is so talented. She's making   e. wheelies.
5. Ken's always popping   f. camping.

Grammar – Verb be: Was / Were

1 Write the sentences in past.

0. He's happy with his new phone. *He was happy with his new phone.*
1. I'm cold in the morning. _____
2. We're late for the math exam. _____
3. They're in LA for the weekend. _____
4. It's a good book. _____
5. Your answer is right. _____
6. She's tired after gym class. _____

2 In your notebook, change the sentences in Activity 1 to negative.

0. *He wasn't happy with his new phone.*

3 Complete and answer the questions.

0. *Was* I in your class? Yes, *you were.*
1. _____ your parents on vacation last week?
   No, they _____.
2. _____ your photo in Facebook?
   No, it _____.
3. _____ Laura and Marta on your camping trip?
   Yes, they _____.
4. _____ you at the swimming pool? No, we _____.
5. _____ your sister on TV last week? Yes, she _____.
6. _____ it hot yesterday? Yes, it _____.

Short Answers

Were you happy?
Yes, I was.
No, I wasn't.

4 Circle and correct one mistake in each sentence.

0. It was Tuesday (tomorrow).
   It was Tuesday yesterday.
1. Was we at your party last week?
   _____
2. My brother weren't at his music lesson.
   _____
3. There wasn't any people at the bus stop yesterday.
   _____
4. Jim and Emmy was in the living room.
   _____
5. There were a great program on TV last night.
   _____

Guess What!
yesterday, today tomorrow

Unit 5

5 Look and complete the sentences with there was / wasn't or there were / weren't.

Dear Diary,
Our last vacation was horrible. The hotel room was the worst in the world!
(0) __There was__ one room for my brother and me. It was terrible!
(1) _____ two beds, but
(2) _____ any chairs and
(3) _____ a table.
(4) _____ a bathroom in the room! It was down the hall.
(5) _____ only one very small window!
(6) _____ soda cans on the floor! (7) _____ also mosquitoes everywhere. It was very hot, but (8) _____ any air conditioning. Unfortunately, (9) _____ another hotel in town, so we were there for a week. It wasn't a hotel—it was a prison!

Review

1 Look at the picture and write sentences.

0. (Saturday) It was a Saturday.
1. (birthday party) _____
2. (cake) _____
3. (gifts) _____
4. (rock music) _____
5. (soda) _____

Reading

1 Read the article and label the people in the pictures.

Carrie Dana George Hugh Jeremy Jess Louise Luke Tom

100th anniversary!

About   Lifestyle   Homes   News

Yesterday was the 100th anniversary of our town. There was a festival and a big street party. The **weather** was amazing and there were hundreds of visitors. It was a great day for everyone. Were you there? Post your pictures below!

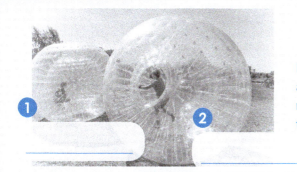

Here are Hugh and me at the festival. We're **zorbing**! It's amazing! You sit in this big ball. They fill it with air and then you roll around like a hamster in a ball. It was fun. I'm on the right at the front of the picture and Hugh is on the left. –Luke

This is the skating competition! I'm rollerblading in the front of the picture and my friend Tom is on the left. Louise is on her skateboard on the right. It was so cool. I wasn't first. That was Tom. I was second. But next year… –Jess

What a way to end the festival! I'm camping with my family. I'm on the right and Jeremy, my father, is on the left. My little sister Dana is in the middle. We're eating **marshmallows**. It's a type of candy and you put it in a fire. My other sister Carrie is holding some next to me. She loves marshmallows. I want to do it all again in another hundred years! –George

2 Read the article again and circle *T* (True) or *F* (False).

1. It was cold at the festival. T F
2. There were a lot of people at the festival. T F
3. People carry hamsters when they are zorbing. T F
4. The competition was only for rollerblading. T F
5. The winner of the skating competition was a girl. T F
6. They are eating meat at the campsite. T F

Glossary

weather: the temperature or conditions outside

zorbing: an activity in which someone rolls in a large transparent plastic ball

marshmallow: a soft white candy

Unit 6

Vocabulary – The Scientific Method

1 Unscramble the sentences and decode the message.

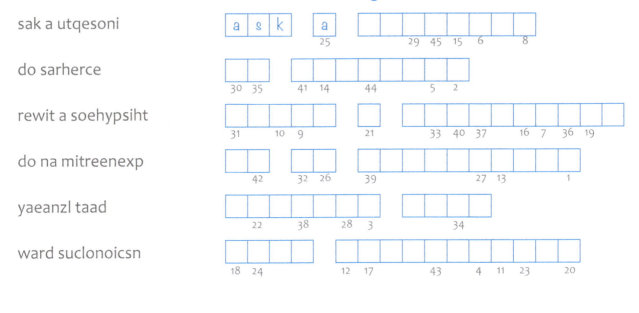

2 Number the sentences according to the scientific method.

- [1] My pet mice liked to chew on limes. I noticed they grew larger than regular mice.
- [ ] I prepared two groups of mice for my experiment. The first group got vitamin C in their diet. The other didn't.
- [ ] Vitamin C does not make mice grow.
- [ ] After two weeks, I weighed the mice in each group and recorded the information. I compared the numbers and noticed that their size was exactly the same.
- [ ] I went online and read about mice, their diet and the effects of vitamin C.
- [ ] I think that if we give vitamin C to mice, they will grow bigger.

3 Write the missing words.

0. I was very nervous ____about____ the final exam!
1. We're _____ with our homework assignments. We can't go.
2. What sport are you good _____?
3. She's _____ about the weekend. She's going to the beach.
4. Jimmy's interested _____ chemistry.
5. You look upset. What are you _____ about?

Grammar – Past Simple

1 Complete the story using the past simple.

I (0) __had__ (have) a strange dream last night. I was in the Amazon. Suddenly, I (1) _____ (see) a snake. I was scared so I (2) _____ (run) into the jungle to escape. I (3) _____ (walk) for a long time. I (4) _____ (feel) very hot. Then I (5) _____ (discover) a waterfall. I (6) _____ (decide) to go into the waterfall and it was very cool. Then, when I (7) _____ (wake) up, I was in the shower! My mom was so angry!

2 Complete the chart using the verbs in Activity 1.

Regular	Irregular
	had

3 Find and write eleven irregular verbs in the past simple.

```
G G H A D P N U L T
B B Y X Z D W F F D
Y E L I D W C O E U
D G C O M R T N F W
R A B A S O A C M Z
O N D F M T K E Q R
V E G Q F E T A H K
E X Q U M S P O K E
```

0. __lost__
1. _____
2. _____
3. _____
4. _____
5. _____
6. _____
7. _____
8. _____
9. _____
10. _____
11. _____

6 Unit

4 Cross out the mistakes and then correct them.

0. I ho~~peed to~~ see you yesterday. _____hoped_____

1. My grandma smileed at me. _____
2. My baby sister cryed all night. _____
3. She tiped the waiter. _____
4. Clara eraseed the board. _____
5. My brother joged in the park. _____
6. I tryied on a new dress for the party. _____

Spelling

Some verbs need spelling changes in simple past.
c + y: study → stud**ied**
v + y: play → play**ed**
e: decide → decid**ed**
Verbs with a c + v + c combination.
ban → ba**nn**ed

c = consonant   v = vowel

5 Complete the conversation with the past simple of the verbs in parentheses.

(0) ___Did you hear___ (you / hear) about the electric unicycle?
No I didn't. What is it?
It's a single wheel and you stand on it and move around. They (1) _____ (invent) it in 2011. I (2) _____ (use) one for the first time last weekend. Look!
What (3) _____ (it / feel) like?
It (4) _____ (feel) really strange in the beginning. Everyone (5) _____ (look) at me when I (6) _____ (go) down the street on it.
(7) _____ (you / fall) off it?
No, I (8) _____ (not / fall) off it. It wasn't very fast. But there was the problem with the police…
(9) _____ (the police / see) you?
Yes, they did. A police officer (10) _____ (ask) me for my driver's license! I'm only 13! Luckily my mom was there and she (11) _____ (speak) to the police officer. It was all OK.
Phew! Lucky for you!

Review

1 Answer the questions about a great vacation you had.

1. Where did you go? _____
2. Did you spend the day with your friends or family?

   _____

3. What did you do? _____
4. What did you eat? _____
5. Did you take any pictures?

   _____

6. What did you take pictures of?

   _____

Reading

1 Read the text and complete the fact file on Robert Louis Stevenson.

Robert Louis Stevenson

Robert Louis Stevenson was the author of *Treasure Island*. He wrote the novel in 1881 – 1882. Readers loved this story of the discovery of buried treasure. His most famous character, Long John Silver, first appeared in *Treasure Island*, and the pirate captain is still one of the most iconic figures in British literature today.

Stevenson also wrote *Strange Case of Doctor Jekyll and Mister Hyde*. In this horror story, Dr. Jekyll changed into a terrible monster after he did a disastrous experiment with some chemicals. Stevenson got the inspiration for his classic novel from a dream.

Robert Louis Stevenson was born in Scotland in 1850. He studied engineering at the University of Edinburgh. Then he worked as a writer all his life. He travelled all over the world. Eventually, the writer decided to live in Samoa in the Pacific Ocean. Unfortunately, he never had good health and he died there in 1894 at the age of 44.

Born (year, place): _____

Education: _____

Famous books: _____

_____

_____

Famous characters: _____

Died (year, place): _____

2 Read the text again and circle T (True) or F (False).

1. Stevenson wrote *Treasure Island* quickly.   T   F
2. Dr. Jekyll was a scientist.   T   F
3. Stevenson studied English literature at university.   T   F
4. Stevenson got the ideas for his stories when he was in bed.   T   F
5. Stevenson was an adventurer.   T   F
6. Stevenson lived a long time.   T   F

Writing

1 Write a one-paragraph biography of an author you like in your notebook. Use these notes to help you.

When was the author born? Where?

When did the author write his / her most famous book?

When did the author's most famous character first appear?

What other books did the author write?

If the author is dead, when did he / she die?

Unit 7

Vocabulary – Weather

1 Find 6 weather words in the word snake.

2 Write the missing letters to complete the weather words.

Seven Fun Facts about the Weather

0. **Snow** isn't always white. High in the mountains snow is sometimes pink because it contains red algae!

1. The fastest w___d ever recorded was in Australia. It moved at 408 kilometers per hour!

2. Visitors to San Francisco often cannot see the famous Golden Gate Bridge, because the city has lots of f____!

3. Arica in Chile is one of the driest places on earth. Once it didn't have r____n for 14 years!

4. In Norway in summer, they have s____ 24 hours a day. It's light all day and all night too!

5. If you see green cl____ds in the sky, go to a safe place quickly! They turn from white to green before a tornado!

6. In a s____rm, you hear thunder and you see lighting. Lightning doesn't just come down from the sky—it also travels up from the ground.

3 Complete the messages with the words below.

cloudy   foggy   rainy   snowy   ~~stormy~~   sunny   windy

#weather

0. I hear bad #weather coming! It'll be _____stormy_____ this afternoon!   17 min

1. It's so _____ today! My clothes are wet. My hair's wet. Even my socks are wet! #weather   19 min

2. It's warm and dry today, but it's not a good idea to go to the beach because it's a bit _____. #weather   25 min

3. It's so _____ today! They canceled our soccer game. We couldn't see the other players! #weather   32 min

4. The penguins at the zoo are happy because it's _____ today, just like in the Antarctic! #weather   50 min

5. It's summer. Time to enjoy the beach because it's _____! #weather   52 min

6. Our boat moved really fast today at sea because of the _____ weather. #weather   57 min

> 150

Grammar – Future: Will and Going to

1 Complete the conversation using future with *will*.

I'm nervous. It's my first day at my new school tomorrow in this new city.

Don't worry, Wendy. You (0) __will be__ (be) OK.

I don't have any friends there. I (1) _____ (not / know) anyone in my class.

You (2) _____ (meet) lots of people, and you (3) _____ (make) some new friends.

Maybe the other kids (4) _____ (not / like) me.

Don't be silly! Look, you (5) _____ (not / be) the only new student in the school. Lots of people (6) _____ (start) school on the same day as you.

You're right. OK.

I'm sure your teacher (7) _____ (help) you too. Keep calm and carry on!

2 Use the words to make predictions.

0. A: My dad bought a a new car!
   B: Yes, but (he / not / lend / you) Yes, but he won't lend it to you.

1. A: I told my secret to Jennifer.
   B: It's OK. (she / not / tell / anyone) _____

2. A: My cat looks sick. I don't know what to do.
   B: (the / vet / know / what's wrong) _____

3. A: Are there any photos of you online? Google yourself!
   B: (you / not / find / any pictures / of me) _____

4. A: I'm worried about this dress for my aunt's wedding.
   B: Why? (everyone / love / it) _____

5. A: I'm a Gemini and so are you. What does our horoscope say?
   B: (we / win / a lot / money / the future) _____

3 Complete the future plans using *going to*. There's an extra verb you don't need.

not be   dance   not make   play   sing   not speak   ~~take~~

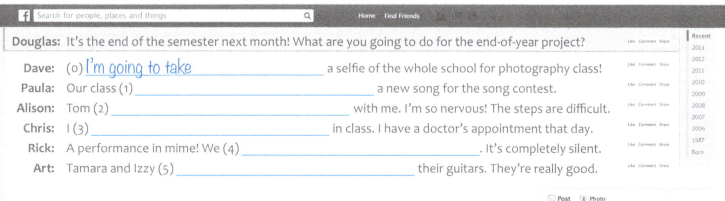

Douglas: It's the end of the semester next month! What are you going to do for the end-of-year project?
Dave: (0) I'm going to take a selfie of the whole school for photography class!
Paula: Our class (1) _____ a new song for the song contest.
Alison: Tom (2) _____ with me. I'm so nervous! The steps are difficult.
Chris: I (3) _____ in class. I have a doctor's appointment that day.
Rick: A performance in mime! We (4) _____. It's completely silent.
Art: Tamara and Izzy (5) _____ their guitars. They're really good.

7 Unit

4 Look at the form and answer the questions in your notebook.

Oldwater Creek Summer Camp

Name: Crystal Jenkins
Month: July

Courses		Sports		Other activities	
Chinese	✓	Baseball	✓	Kayaking	✓
Spanish	☐	Soccer	☐	Horse riding	✓
		Volleyball	☐	Theater	☐

0. When is Crystal going to attend summer camp?
   She's going to be there in July.
1. Which language is she going to learn?
2. Which sport is she going to play?
3. Is she going to go kayaking?
4. What other activities is she going to do?
5. Is she going to do everything at the summer camp?

5 Cross out one extra word in each dialogue.
0. A: ~~Do~~ will it be stormy tomorrow?
   B: Yes, it will.
1. A: Will we to have snow on the weekend?
   B: Yes, we will.
2. A: Will you live in the US after you leave school?
   B: No, I don't won't.
3. A: What time is our train be going to leave?
   B: At 3 p.m.
4. A: Are you going to help me with my model?
   B: No, I'm no not.
5. A: Is Gemma going to stay at your house tomorrow?
   B: Yes, she's is.

Short Answers

Use the auxiliary in short answers.

Will it rain?
  Yes, it **will**. / No, it **won't**.

Are you **going to** eat?
  Yes, I **am**. / No, I'm **not**.

152 Review

1 Look at this weekly planner. Write sentences in your notebook.

Weekly planner

Monday	Tuesday	Wednesday	Thursday	Friday	Saturday	Sunday
buy new phone.	take dog to vet	go to library	English test	rollerblading with friends	go swimming with friends	visit grandparents

0. *I'm going to buy a new phone on Monday.*

Reading

1 Look at the pictures and the titles. Mark (✓) a–d if you think the article will mention them. Then read and check.

a. ☐ Different types of rainbow.
b. ☐ Rainbows in art.
c. ☐ The history of the rainbow.
d. ☐ The science of rainbows.

The Amazing World of Rainbows

¹ "Red and yellow and pink and green, purple, orange and blue," goes the old song. It's a way of remembering the seven colors of the rainbow, but in fact, rainbows are made of millions of colors, not just seven. Only about a hundred of these are visible to the human eye.

² Rainbows fascinated **ancient** people, just like today, and there are lots of **legends** about them. In one, you will find gold at the end of a rainbow.

³ Rainbows appear when light from the sun travels through rain at exactly 42°. Most rainbows appear in the morning and in the evening when the light is perfect.

⁴ It is possible to see a double or even a triple rainbow. Most amazing of all is the fogbow. This very rare event happens when the sunlight moves through cloud or fog. Fogbows are larger than normal rainbows, but the colors are not very bright.

⁵ When it's sunny, you can make your own rainbow. Get a glass of water and a piece of white paper. Stand near a window. Put the glass above the paper. The light makes a rainbow on the paper!

2 Match the information with the paragraph in the article. There is an extra option.

- ③ When to see rainbows
- ☐ Rainbows in bad weather
- ☐ Why they are called rainbows
- ☐ Part of a rainbow is invisible
- ☐ An experiment that you can do at home
- ☐ An old rainbow myth

Glossary
ancient: very old
legend: a very old story

Unit 8

Vocabulary – Feelings

1 Write the missing letters to complete the words.

Tech News   February 27

Emojis Everywhere

by Roy Lawrence

Beep Beep! An (0) e __x__ c __i__ t __e__ d face appears on your phone. Immediately you know it's good news. It's simple. It's easy. It's emoji—the world's fastest growing language.

Emoji comes from Japan, where "e" means picture and "moji" means character. It's a simple way of communicating an idea, like a face with a big open mouth, that means "I'm (1) f r _____ t e n e d". The very first example of emojis was the smiley face. Scott Fahlman of Carnegie Mellon University invented the simple :-) (2) h _____ y face in 1982 and he also invented :-(to show you're (3) s _____. These early designs were surprisingly inventive, especially the (4) a _____ r _____ face >:-(and it took thirty years for technology to catch up.

Emoticons are still not perfect because they're not always completely transparent. For example,

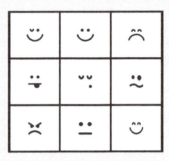

Emojis, the new way to express emotions

do people send a green face because they feel sick or (5) j _____ o _____ s?

The other problem is that teachers are (6) w _____ r i _____ that young people are forgetting how to communicate. There are even reports of students writing emoticons on exams. Kids obviously won't make these errors as adults, but for now, they might need an (7) e _____ b _____ r _____ s e d face when their teachers tell them about the mistake.

Emojis are part of everyday texting.

2 Cross out the word that doesn't belong.

0. excited
happy
~~sad~~

1. angry
excited
jealous

2. frightened
sad
worried

3. worried
sad
excited

4. angry
embarrassed
worried

5. angry
happy
frightened

3 Complete the sentences with the noun forms of the words in parentheses.

0. The weather is my main _____worry_____ (worried) about the camping trip.

1. Before the concert, you could feel the _____ (excited) in the audience.

2. People don't like you because you're successful. It's pure _____ (jealous).

3. I don't like tragedies. There is enough _____ (sad) in the real world.

4. In any sport, it's important to control your _____ (angry).

5. There was a photo of me in a newspaper, but to my _____ (embarrassed) it had my sister's name on it!

6. For me, _____ (happy) is spending time with my friends.

Grammar – Questions

1 Complete the interview using the questions.

- Why do you like it?
- What is your favorite TV show?
- What is it about?
- How long is the show?
- When did it start?
- Who are the actors in it?

(0) **Q:** What is your favorite TV show?
   A: It's Doctor Who.
(1) **Q:** _____
   A: The Doctor is an alien. He travels in space and time.
(2) **Q:** _____
   A: In 1963. It's the oldest sci-fi show on TV in the world. It's still running today.
(3) **Q:** _____
   A: The doctor can change his appearance, so lots of different people play the role.
(4) **Q:** _____
   A: I'm always excited when it starts because you never know where the doctor will be.
(5) **Q:** _____
   A: It's normally 45 minutes, but sometimes the stories are in two episodes.

2 Write yes/no questions.

0. you / watching / TV / right / now?
   Are you watching TV right now?
1. Hank / going / visit / us / tomorrow?
   _____
2. Tom / usually / do / judo / after school?
   _____
3. your mom / drive / you / to / school / yesterday?
   _____
4. the / baby / sleeping / at / the moment?
   _____
5. be / there / any / milk / in / the / fridge?
   _____

Unit 8

3 Circle the correct options to complete the conversation.

Mom: (0) **What** / Which do you want to do?
Brian: Have a snack and a drink.
Mom: OK. Here's a drink.
Vicky: (1) What / Which one is mine: the red or the blue cup?
Mom: They're the same.
Vicky: (2) What / Which one do you prefer, Brian?
Brian: I don't mind.
Vicky: OK. I'll have the red one.
Mom: (3) What / Which do you want to eat?
Brian: (4) What / Which do we have?
Mom: Well… we have some muffins. One's strawberry and one's chocolate.
(5) What / Which muffin would you like?
Vicky: Chocolate.
Brian: Vicky, you always want the chocolate one! I want it, too!
Mom: OK. Brian, cut the chocolate muffin in half and share it with your sister.
Brian: All right. Here you are. (6) What / Which half do you want? Left or right?
Vicky: Left.
Brian: I knew it! The biggest one!
Vicky: (7) What / Which do you expect? You cut it, Brian!

Review

1 Read the messages and say how the people are feeling.

twitter

Sheila
I'm the only person working on my school project! The other people in my group aren't doing anything!
30 minutes ago

Aaron
My parents put a photo of me as a baby on Facebook. Now everyone is laughing at me!
1 hour ago

Emilio
We're going to the US for the first time ever tomorrow! San Diego! I can't wait!
2 hours ago

Lisa
Jackie's parents buy her new clothes all the time, but my parents never buy me anything. She's so lucky and I'm unlucky.
3 hours ago

Walt
There was a small earthquake yesterday. What if there's a big one tomorrow? I don't want to go out because it's too dangerous.
3 hours ago

Atsuko
And now the school vacation begins! Eight weeks with no school, no exams, no homework, just fun, fun, fun!
4 hours ago

0. *Sheila's angry.*
1. _____
2. _____
3. _____
4. _____
5. _____

Writing

1 Read the book review. How many stars does the review give the book?

70 of 120 people found the following review helpful
★★★
By **Ramon Blanco**
Verified purchase (What's this?)

This review is for: **The Adventures of Tintin – The Black Island**

I discovered Tintin through the 2011 movie by Steven Spielberg. Tintin is a young newspaper reporter who investigates mysteries around the world. The comics were very popular and there are over twenty books, all by writer/artist Hergé. I wanted to know more so I bought one online: *The Black Island*.

The Black Island is a mystery in Scotland. Tintin encounters a mysterious plane in Belgium. He offers to help, but the pilot attacks him. The plane escapes to Britain. Tintin is suspicious, so he follows them to Scotland. He knows they are criminals, but what are they doing?

The artwork is amazing. All the characters have very simple faces, but they show lots of emotion. The pictures of scenery are incredible, and I really love the cover.

The only problem is that the book is from 1966 and there are lots of things that look old. There is no Internet and there are no phones. The cars look like antiques, so it is not like a modern comic at all.

The Black Island is a fun introduction to the Tintin books. It is also a very good way to practice your English because when there are new words, the pictures help you understand what they mean. I think it's a very good book.

Was this review helpful to you? Yes No

Add a comment

2 Mark (✓) the correct options.

0. Ramon
   a. ✓ is a recent fan of Tintin.
   b. ☐ is not a fan of Tintin.
   c. ☐ was always a fan of Tintin.

1. *The Black Island* is
   a. ☐ an adventure story.
   b. ☐ a comedy.
   c. ☐ science fiction.

2. Ramon thinks the illustrations are
   a. ☐ complicated.
   b. ☐ excellent.
   c. ☐ strange.

3. The purpose of the fourth paragraph is
   a. ☐ to criticize the book.
   b. ☐ to laugh at the book.
   c. ☐ to explain why the book is popular.

4. Ramon recommends the book for
   a. ☐ children.
   b. ☐ everyone.
   c. ☐ language learners.

3 Write a review of a comic book, graphic novel or book. Use this plan to help you.
- paragraph 1: why you read it
- paragraph 2: the plot (no spoilers!)
- paragraph 3: the artwork (if it is a comic or graphic novel)
- paragraph 4: any problems with the book
- paragraph 5: conclusion. Who would like the book?

Just for Fun Answer Key

Unit 1
1 *From top to bottom*: math, music, Spanish, literature, geography, chemistry, art, technology, history
My favorite subject: physical education
2 *From top to bottom*: have, makes, sleep, helps, eats, studies
3 a recorder
4 a river

Unit 2
1 1. waiting 2. baking 3. eating 4. raining 5. *Down*: sleeping *Across*: swimming 6. running 7. dancing 8. traveling
2 *From top to bottom*: engineer → safety helmet, safety goggles; firefighter → hose, boots; hairstylist → blow dryer, comb; pilot → jacket, hat; receptionist → bell, computer; transit operator → train ticket, dashboard

Unit 3
1 *Top row*: 2nd picture and *Bottom row*: 1st picture
2 *Shoe sizes*: Sean – 6, Matt – 9, Tim – 7, Mike – 10, Roy – 8
3 1. inbox 2. Robin Hood

Unit 4
1 *Countable*: oranges, cherries, tomatoes, carrots, potatoes, onions
Uncountable: sugar, milk, flour, bread, coffee, oil
2 1. chipmunk 2. horse 3. chameleon 4. goldfish

Unit 5
1 1. camping 2. doing cannonballs 3. hanging out 4. popping a wheelie 5. making models 6. playing board games 7. rollerblading 8. dancing 9. drawing
2 1. desert 2. Arabic 3. camel 4. Bedouin 5. Saudi Arabia 6. Friday
3 1. Bedouin 2. Saudi Arabia 3. Arabic 4. desert 5. camel 6. Friday

Unit 6
1 1. question 2. research 3. hypothesis 4. experiment 5. analyze 6. conclusions
2 1. begin – began 2. discover – discovered 3. hear – heard 4. write – wrote
3 bacteria
4 Give me a ring sometime!

Unit 7
1 *Clockwise from the top left*: storm, snow, rain, cloud, fog, sun, wind
2 1. snowy 2. windy 3. foggy 4. sunny 5. rainy 6. stormy 7. cloudy
3 1. c 2. d 3. e 4. b 5. a

Unit 8
1 *From top to bottom*: jealous, sad, worried, embarrassed, happy, angry, excited, frightened
Mystery feeling: curious
2 1. will 2. What 3. this 4. do 5. you 6. afternoon
Mystery question: What will you do this afternoon?
3 your reflection

Grammar Reference

Unit 1

Present Simple

We use the present simple to talk about routines, repeated actions and general truths.
- *I **get up** early.*

In affirmative sentences for *I, you, we, they*, we use the base form of the verb.
- *I **live** in a small town.*
- *You **have** brown eyes.*
- *We **go** to the movies.*
- *They **play** video games.*

In affirmative sentences for *he, she, it*, we add –s or –es to the verb.
- *She **eats** breakfast.*
- *He **does** his homework.*

To make negative sentences, we use the auxiliary verb *don't* for *I, you, we, they*, or *doesn't* for *he, she, it*, and the base form of the verb.
- *They **don't play** video games.*
- *She **doesn't eat** breakfast.*

To make questions, we use the auxiliary verb *do* for *I, you, we, they* or *does* for *he, she, it*, and the base form of the verb.
- ***Do** they **play** video games?*
- ***Does** she **eat** breakfast?*

For short answers to Yes/No questions, you omit the verb and use the auxiliary verb.
- ***Do** they **play** video games?*
  *Yes, they **do**. / No, they **don't**.*
- ***Does** she **eat** breakfast?*
  *Yes, she **does**. / No, she **doesn't**.*

To ask for specific information, we use wh– words.
- ***Where** do you live?*
- ***What** do they do?*
- ***What** does she eat?*
- ***Who** does he go to the movies with?*
- ***When** do we have math class?*

Adverbs of Frequency

We use adverbs of frequency to say how often we do an activity.
- *I **always** get up early. (100%)*
- *He **usually** does his homework. (75%)*
- *We **often** go to the movies. (50%)*
- *They **sometimes** play video games. (25%)*
- *She **never** eats meat. (0%)*

We usually put the adverb of frequency before the verb, but *sometimes* can also go at the beginning of a sentence.
- ***Sometimes**, they play video games.*

To ask questions, we use *ever* or *How often*. *How often* goes at the beginning, and *ever* goes before the verb.
- *Do you **ever** get up late?*
  *No, I **never** get up late.*
- ***How often** do they play video games?*
  *They **sometimes** play video games.*

Prepositions

We use prepositions of time (*in, at, on*) to say when actions happen.
- *He does his homework **in the afternoon**.*
- *She doesn't study **at night**.*
- *We go to the movies **on Saturdays**.*
- *They go on vacation **in July**.*

SEPTEMBER						
Sun	Mon	Tue	Wed	Thu	Fri	Sat
28	29	30	31	1	2	3
4	5	6	7	8	9	10
11	12	13	14	15	16	17
18	19	20	21	22	23	24
25	26	27	28	29	30	1

Unit 2

Present Continuous

We use the present continuous to talk about activities that are happening now.
- I **am walking** to school.

We form the present continuous with the verb *be* in the present simple, and the base form of the verb with –ing.
- He **is going** to karate class.
- She **is helping** people.
- We **are doing** our homework.
- They **are building** robots.

To make negative sentences, we add *not* (n't) to the verb *be*.
- He **isn't going** to karate class.
- They **aren't building** robots.

To form Yes/No questions, we put the verb *be* before the subject.
- **Is** he **going** to karate class?
- **Are** they **building** robots?

For short answers to Yes/No questions, we use the verb *be*.
- **Is** he **going** to karate class?
  Yes, he **is**. / No, he **isn't**.
- **Are** they **building** robots?
  Yes, they **are**. / No, they **aren't**.

To ask for information, we use *wh–* words.
- **Where** is he going?
- **Why** are they building robots?
- **Who** is walking to school?
- **What** is she doing?

Prepositions

We use prepositions of place (*on, at, in*) to say where actions happen. We use *on* to talk about public transportation, *at* for buildings, and *in* for geographical areas or rooms in a building.

- He's reading a book **on** the bus.

- They're working out **at** the gym.

- We live **in** New York City.

- She's eating lunch **in** the cafeteria.

Unit 3

Comparatives

We use comparatives to talk about the differences between two people, places or things.
- She is **younger than** her brother.
- L.A. is **smaller than** New York City.
- A laptop is **more expensive than** a tablet.

Short adjectives are one-syllable or two-syllable adjectives (which end in –y).
- She is **young**.
- They are **funny**.

We form the comparative of short adjectives by adding –er followed by *than*.
- She is **younger than** he is.
- They are **taller than** we are.

For short adjectives ending in a vowel + consonant, double the consonant before adding –er.
- New York City is **bigger than** L.A.

If a short adjective ends in a consonant + –y, it becomes –ier in the comparative form.
- They are **funnier than** we are.
- My room is **messier than** my brother's.

Long adjectives can have two or three syllables.
- That mall is **modern**.
- He is **serious**.
- A car is **expensive**.

We form the comparative of long adjectives by using *more* + adjective + *than*.
- That mall is **more modern than** this one.
- He is **more serious than** his sister.
- A car is **more expensive than** a bike.

Exceptions to the rules: *good* and *bad*.
- **Good** → Better
- He thinks pizza is **better than** pasta.
- **Bad** → Worse
- The pollution in big cities is **worse than** the pollution in small towns.

Superlatives

We use the superlative form of an adjective when we are comparing more than two things or people.
- She is **the youngest** person in our class.
- They are **the most polite** students in our school.

We form the superlative of short adjectives by adding –est to the adjective.
- He is **the tallest** player on the team.
- That is **the cheapest** computer in the store.

For short adjectives ending in vowel + consonant, double the consonant before adding –est.
- New York City is **the biggest** city in the USA.

If a short adjective ends in a consonant + –y, it becomes –iest in the superlative form.
- They are **the funniest** students in our school.
- My room is **the messiest** in the house.

We form the superlative of long adjectives by using *most* + adjective.
- That is **the most modern** mall in this city.
- He is **the most serious** person we know.
- That car is **the most expensive** one here.

Exceptions to the rules: *good* and *bad*.
- **Good** → The best
- He thinks pizza is **the best** food in the world.
- **Bad** → The worst
- That city has **the worst** pollution in the country.

Unit 4

Countable and Uncountable Nouns

Countable nouns are objects we can count, such as *strawberries*, *apples* and *books*.

Countable nouns can be singular or plural. We use the articles *a* and *an* with countable nouns.
- I had **an apple** for lunch.
- I like **apples**.

We can't count uncountable nouns. They have no plural form, but it is possible to count them and measure them with weights or volume.
- He usually drinks **two liters of water** a day.
- The recipe calls for **a cup of sugar**.

Quantifiers

To talk about amounts, we use quantifiers: *a little*, *a few*, *some*, *a lot (of)* and *not any*.

For countable nouns, we use *not any*, *a few*, *some*, and *a lot (of)*.
- There **aren't any** apples in the refrigerator.
- I need **a few** carrots for the soup.
- Please buy **some** onions at the store.
- The library has **a lot of** books.

For uncountable nouns, we use *not any*, *a little*, *some*, and *a lot (of)*.
- There **isn't any** flour.
- She puts **a little** sugar in her coffee.
- You need to put **some** cheese on the sandwiches.
- There's **a lot of** salt in this soup!

We use *how many* to ask about the amount of countable nouns, and *how much* to ask about the amount of uncountable nouns.
- **How many** potatoes do we need?
- **How much** salt should we put in the soup?

Verb be: was, were

The past form of the verb *be* takes two forms: *was* or *were*.

We use *was* with *I, he, she* and *it*.
- I **was** sad yesterday.
- He **was** five years old in this picture.
- She **was** a very serious student.
- It **was** very cold last week.

We use *were* with *you, we* and *they*.
- You **were** late to class last Tuesday.
- We **were** excited about the new movie.
- They **were** in the library.

To make negative sentences, we add *not*.
- I **was not** happy yesterday.
- They **were not** in the cafeteria.

The contractions of *was not* and *were not* are:
- **wasn't**
  I **wasn't** happy yesterday.
- **weren't**
  They **weren't** in the cafeteria.

To form Yes/No questions, we put the verb *be* before the subject.
- **Was** she a serious student?
- **Were** they in the library?

For short answers to Yes/No questions, we use the past simple of *be*.
- **Was** she a serious student?
  Yes, she **was**. / No, she **wasn't**.
- **Were** they in the library?
  Yes, they **were**. / No, they **weren't**.

To ask for information, we use *wh–* words.
- **Who** was last to class last Tuesday?
- **Where** were they yesterday?
- **When** were you sad?

There was / There were

We use *there was* or *there were* to talk about what existed in the past.

We use *there was* with singular nouns.
- **There was** a map in the classroom.

We use *there were* with plural nouns.
- **There were** chairs.

To make negative sentences, we add *not*.
- **There was not (wasn't)** a TV in the classroom.
- **There were not (weren't)** any computers.

To form Yes/No questions, we put *was* or *were* before *there*.
- **Was there** a map in the classroom?
- **Were there** chairs?

For short answers, we use:
- Yes, **there was**. / No, **there wasn't**.
- Yes, **there were**. / No, **there weren't**.

164

Unit 6

Past Simple

We use the past simple to talk about a completed action that took place at a definite moment in the past.
- He **painted** the walls in his room.
- We **wore** uniforms to schools.

Verbs in the past simple can be regular or irregular.

Past Simple (Regular verbs, Affirmative)

Most regular verbs end in –ed in affirmative sentences in the past simple.
- I **worked** last night.
- We **asked** questions in class.

If a regular verb ends in consonant + –y, it changes to –ied in the past simple.
- She **studied** yesterday.

If it's a one-syllable verb and ends in consonant + vowel + consonant (and not in –w or –y), we double the last consonant and add –ed.
- They **stopped** at the store.
- She **shopped** at the mall.

Past Simple (Irregular verbs, Affirmative)

Irregular verbs in the past simple take several different forms.
- She **did** her homework on the weekend.
- We **went** to the movies last night.

To study the irregular verb forms, use the *Verb List* on page 168.

Past Simple (Negative)

For both regular and irregular verbs we use *did not* (*didn't*) and the verb in base form.
- He **didn't paint** the outside of the house.
- She **didn't do** her homework.

Past Simple (Questions)

To make *Yes/No* questions we put the auxiliary *Did* before the subject. We use the base form of the verb.
- **Did** he **paint** the walls in his room?
- **Did** she **do** her homework?

To answer *Yes/No* questions, we use the auxiliary *did* or *didn't*. We don't use the verb.
- **Did** he **paint** the walls in his room? Yes, he **did**. / No, he **didn't**.
- **Did** she **do** her homework? Yes, she **did**. / No, she **didn't**.

Unit 7

Future: *will*

We use future simple to talk about predictions based on personal opinion.
- I **will learn** to drive next year.
- It **will rain** tomorrow.

In affirmative sentences, we use the auxiliary *will* and a verb.
- He **will help** people.
- We **will do** our homework.

To make negative sentences, we add *not* to the auxiliary *will*. *Won't* is the contraction of *will not*.
- He **will not help** people.
- We **won't do** our homework.

To ask Yes/No questions, the auxiliary *will* goes at the beginning.
- **Will** it **rain** tomorrow?
- **Will** you **learn** to drive next year?

For short answers to Yes/No questions, we use the auxiliary *will* or *won't*.
- **Will** it **rain** tomorrow?
  Yes, it **will**. / No, it **won't**.
- **Will** you **learn** to drive next year?
  Yes, I **will**. / No, I **won't**.

Future: *going to*

We use *going to* to talk about plans in the future.
- He **is going to** play the guitar at the party.
- They **are going to** watch movies this weekend.

In affirmative sentences, we use *be* + *going to* + verb.
- I **am going to go** to the café with my friends.
- She **is going to study** in France next year.

To make negative sentences, we add *not* before *going to*.
- I **am not going to go** to the movies.
- She **is not going to study** in Spain next year.

To ask Yes/No questions, we put the verb *be* before the subject.
- **Are** you **going to go** to the café?
- **Is** she **going to study** in France next year?

For short answers to Yes/No questions, we use the verb *be* or the verb *be* + *not*.
- **Are** you **going to go** to the café?
  Yes, I **am**. / No, I **am not**.
- **Is** she **going to study** in France next year?
  Yes, she **is**. / No, she **isn't**.

Questions

We use *wh–* words to ask for information.
- *What* – to ask about an action
- *What* – to ask about an object
- *Where* – to ask about a place or location
- *When* – to ask about a time
- *Who* – to ask about a person
- *How often* – to ask about the frequency of something
- *Which* – to ask about a choice

Present Simple
- **What do** you **do** after school?
- **What do** you **play** after school?
- **Where do** you **take** guitar lessons?
- **When do** you **have** lunch?
- **Who do** you **hang out** with?
- **How often do** you **check** your emails?
- **Which** sandwich **do** you **want**?

Present Continuous

How often and *When* are not usually used in the present continuous.
- **What are** you **doing**?
- **What are** you **watching**?
- **Where are** you **going**?
- **Who are** you **talking** to?

Past Simple
- **What did** you **do** yesterday afternoon?
- **What did** you **see** at the movies last Saturday?
- **Where did** you **find** your keys?
- **When did** you **get** home?
- **Who did** you **hang out** with last summer?
- **How often did** you **go** to the park?
- **Which** bus **did** you **take**?

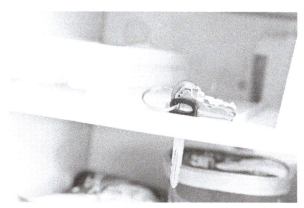

Verb List

Present	Past	Present	Past	Present	Past
analyze	analyzed	give	gave	record	recorded
answer	answered	go	went	remove	removed
appear	appeared	grow	grew	return	returned
arrive	arrived	hang out	hung out	ride	rode
ask	asked	happen	happened	run	ran
be	was / were	have	had	save	saved
become	became	hear	heard	say	said
begin	began	help	helped	see	saw
believe	believed	invent	invented	send	sent
break	broke	investigate	investigated	serve	served
bring	brought	join	joined	sew	sewed
buy	bought	jump	jumped	show	showed
call	called	keep	kept	sing	sang
cancel	canceled	know	knew	sit	sat
carry	carried	laugh	laughed	sleep	slept
choose	chose	learn	learned	solve	solved
come	came	like	liked	speak	spoke
consider	considered	listen	listened	spend	spent
cook	cooked	live	lived	start	started
create	created	look	looked	stay	stayed
dance	danced	lose	lost	stop	stopped
decompose	decomposed	love	loved	study	studied
describe	described	make	made	swim	swam
design	designed	meet	met	take	took
die	died	miss	missed	tell	told
discover	discovered	move	moved	think	thought
discuss	discussed	need	needed	throw	threw
do	did	notice	noticed	travel	traveled
draw	drew	open	opened	try	tried
drink	drank	paint	painted	turn	turned
eat	ate	pay	paid	use	used
encourage	encouraged	pick	picked	visit	visited
enjoy	enjoyed	plant	planted	wait	waited
exercise	exercised	play	played	walk	walked
feel	felt	practice	practiced	want	wanted
find	found	prefer	preferred	watch	watched
finish	finished	prepare	prepared	wear	wore
fly	flew	put	put	win	won
forget	forgot	rain	rained	work	worked
fry	fried	read	read	write	wrote
get	got	receive	received		